DAUMIER

THIS VOLUME, EDITED BY ANDRÉ GLŒCKNER, WAS FIRST PUBLISHED IN NOVEMBER MCMXXXVIII, FOR THE HYPERION PRESS, PARIS. COLOUR BLOCKS ENGRAVED BY CLICHÉS UNION, PARIS, AND PRINTED BY PETIT & CIE, PARIS. PHOTOGRAVURE ENGRAVED BY ÉTABLISSEMENTS JEAN MALVAUX, BRUSSELS, AND PRINTED BY A. HUMBLOT & CIE, NANCY. TEXT AND BINDING BY IMPRIMERIE CRÉTÉ, PARIS.

DAUMIER

BY

JACQUES LASSAIGNE

TRANSLATED FROM THE FRENCH

BY

EVELINE BYAM SHAW

FRENCH AND EUROPEAN PUBLICATIONS, INC.
610, FIFTH AVENUE, NEW-YORK, N. Y.
THE HYPERION PRESS, PARIS

MADE IN FRANCE
COPYRIGHT 1938 BY HYPERION, PARIS

DAUMIER

AS A PAINTER

Head of a Man. Red chalk.
(Claude Roger-Marx collection, Paris.)

Head of a Man.
(Claude Roger-Marx collection, Paris.)

of the essential aspects of his talent. Some of the big private collections are particularly rich in paintings by Daumier; for example the unforgettable, in fact unique, assemblage in the Paul Bureau collection sold in 1927. But these collections are dispersed one after the other, and their most important examples get buried in private possession abroad; their ownership is often anonymous and compelled to remain so, owing to the fact that in certain countries Daumier is considered a subversive artist. A measure of the rate at which this dispersal is progressing is to be found in the difficulty we have had in getting together even photographic records of works all traces of which tend little by little to disappear.

The fact of the matter is that in spite of

It is the first time in France that any work as abundantly illustrated as this has been devoted to Daumier's work as a painter. For sixty years the best writers and art-critics have been attempting to make known the significance and the greatness of one who, as a painter, was completely ignored by the public during his life-time and who since his death has had scarcely any chance of becoming better known, apart from the admirable exhibition of 1934 at the Orangerie. Few artists are so badly represented in the public galleries of France as he is. Even at the Louvre, his work is scattered and badly shown; and though by exhibiting the water-colours and drawings now kept in portfolios it could at least be made fairly representative, it is at present practically impossible to gain even a cursory view

Don Quixote.
(Claude Roger-Marx collection, Paris).

exhibitions and artistic publications, there continues to exist an unmistakable general indifference in the intelligent artistic world with regard to Daumier's work as a painter. Individually, few paintings are so much sought after by collectors and few reach such high prices. But nevertheless the mass of the public, while paying full respect to Daumier as a legend, knows nothing about him as an individual and nothing about his artistic genius. Ready-made ideas, kept in circulation by a few meagre anecdotes, take the place of direct acquaintance. The first prejudice and the one which is still the most firmly rooted, since it has appeared quite recently in the writings of well-known critics, is that Daumier painted only sporadically in oils and had neither the power nor the knowledge to finish a picture. We shall encounter plenty of other prejudices which in the course of this study we shall attempt to destroy. They all arise from the belief that a complete knowledge of Daumier can be obtained from his lithographs. These form among his works a disproportionately long chapter, but it is by no means the final one. It is a chapter in which he was frequently tied down to the exterior world of current events, to the demands of readers and the chance requirements of his text. In his own estimation it formed merely a sort of introduction and preparation for his painting.

It is no part of our purpose to minimise the importance of his printed work. He was undoubtedly the first to make lithography a real art, the first to forge from such poor material a weapon of infinite flexibility. We have no wish to emphasize further the contrast between the different elements of an *œuvre* which has already suffered enough from the very fact of being too seldom considered as a whole. It is quite evident that Daumier's lithographic work, that comedy of manners with so many hundreds of scenes, afforded the artist an inexhaustible repertory of images. By exploring the technical possibilities of lithography his drawing gained an ease of execution, a more concrete sense of volume, and an infinite play of gradations. The experiments in illumination, the effects of light and shade which distinguish so many of his paintings, come as a continuation and completion of the effects he obtained in black and white. The terrible labours which Daumier was compelled to undertake all his life to gain his livelihood, the thousands of stones he worked upon for publishers and readers of the most different possible sorts, who were often of all people the least able to understand him, was not wasted work, and did not remain unfruitful. I feel sure, on the contrary, that his work as a painter gained from it both in depth and freedom; even at the time, Baudelaire, with his infallible gift for prophecy, described the drawing of Daumier's lithographs as irresistibly evocative of the idea of colour. In fact, when Daumier took to painting in oils, he was already in possession of a technique well broken-in to all the exigencies of expression. It was not the technique of a painter; certain works were destined to suffer from mistakes in preparation and Daumier was long to remain faithful to the requirements of black and white owing to his inaptitude in the use of paints, but at least in his paintings there is no lack of experience, no evidence of beginners' work. Almost all of them, though unfinished, retouched, and worked many times over, bear the signs of new experiments in technique and in simplification.

Mountebank.
(Claude Roger-Marx collection, Paris.)

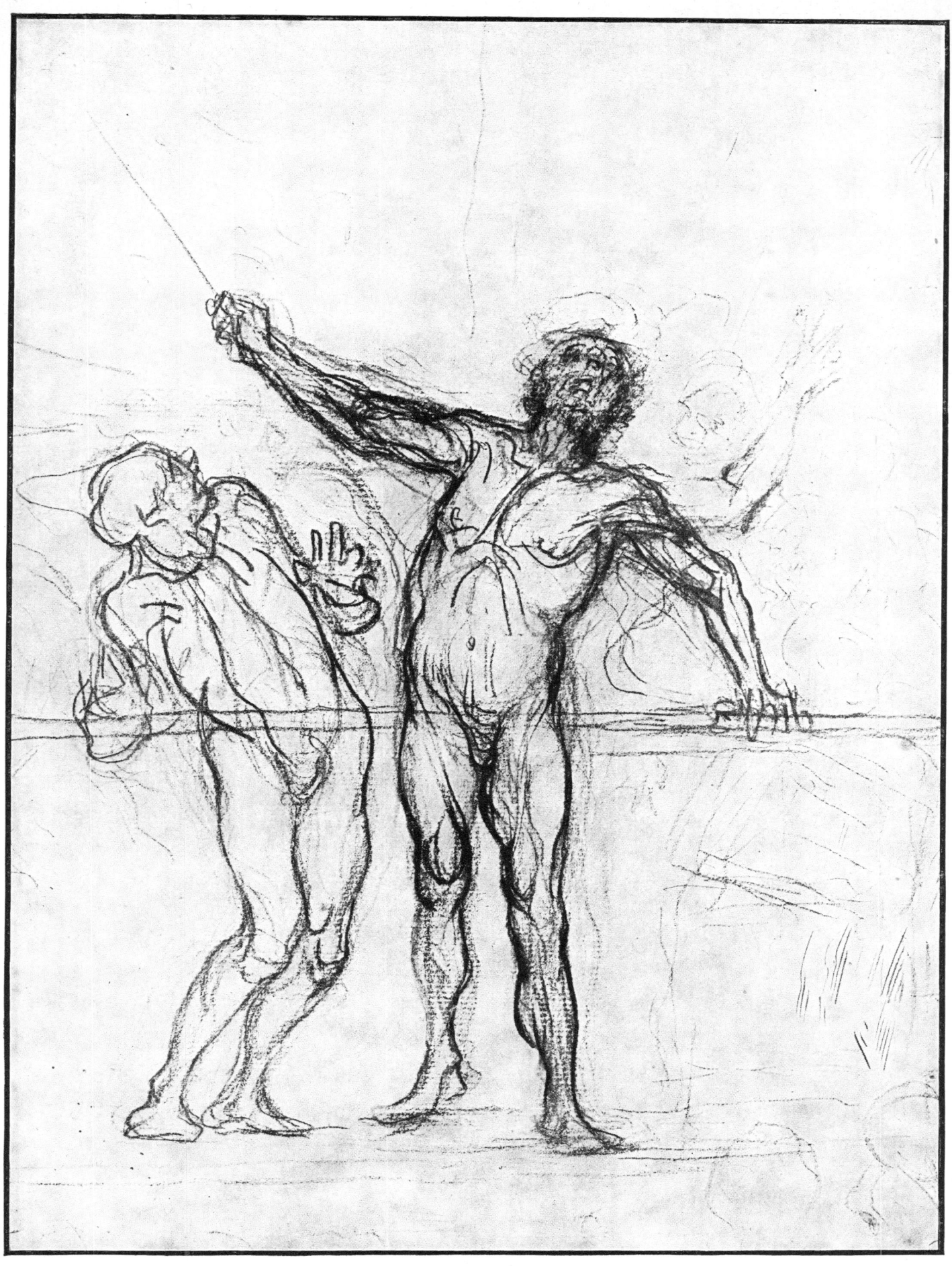

The Show.
(Claude Roger-Marx collection, Paris.)

Sketch.

But their point of departure already represented a high degree of achievement; a world already conquered by his work in lithography lay behind him. This continual triumphant progress is one of the most striking features of Daumier's work. From the first he was master of the technique of lithography. The famous political cartoons of his youth are evidence of a victorious talent. There was to be no falling off; each new plate bore the same stamp of authority; and on the basis of this already finished and perfected work he was to erect a new edifice, an edifice which, even if in the eyes of the world it seems half or unsuccessfully completed, has unquestionably reached heights as lofty as any that the human spirit has attained. The astonishing art that is Daumier's, born, as it were, complete in all its details, wholly detached in its aims, soars miraculously above all notions of time, period and evolution; it moves within the limits of conceptions quite peculiar and personal whose secrets Daumier alone possessed. No transitions connect it with previous works; one looks in vain for influences or repetitions; of a possible successor there is no sign. Regret has often been expressed at the impossibility of dating Daumier's paintings.

Head.
(Claude Roger-Marx collection, Paris.)

In view of the artist's habit of going over his work again and of repeating the same themes *ad infinitum*, the attempt has generally been given up. However, M. Jean Adhémar has pointed out in a learned article that classification would perhaps not be so difficult if a methodical comparison were to be made between the paintings and the lithographs, in which one frequently finds points of similarity. In fact, it has been possible to date a small number of Daumier's works more or less exactly by the use of this method and of the other slight indications which are available. No doubt a microscopic study would give further results, and this theory, which vindicates the claim we have made for the need to consider Daumier's work as a whole, may be taken as serious. However, I myself consider that the problems which this theory attempts to deal with are, in spite of their apparent insolubility, of no importance. The truth is that the dating of Daumier's paintings is not attempted because in their case chronological classification would have no sort of meaning or interest. The painting of Daumier is absolutely isolated; it has neither beginning or end. It might be thought of as a series of concentric variations on parallel themes. Each cycle must be taken by itself and each follows almost exactly the same evolution. Even if it were to be discovered that Daumier had painted each of these cycles one after the other—which is not the case— for instance, if he had painted the Law Courts series before or after the Don Quixote series or the Third Class Carriage scenes, the fact would still remain that these questions of priority are without significance and that each cycle is a world of its own. (Probably this curious fact is explained by

Sketch.
(Claude Roger-Marx collection, Paris.)

Daumier's method of work. He had a tremendous faculty for storing up, retaining and concentrating everything in his head, and he could assimilate it all until there came into being a work of « imagination all compact », summing up anew all outside influences but completely detached from them.)

A sort of natural selection operates in the case of every artist. The best of his work alone survives the course of centuries and even in his life-time a choice work must catch on or perish. But with Daumier it is different; his whole work in oils is in itself a precious entity; it is the essence and residue of a whole life burnt to the last ashes by a sacred flame. All that was dross, all that was unworthy had never even seen the light of day.

Sketch.
(Claude Roger-Marx collection, Paris.)

It is no part of our business to reconstitute the catalogues already in existence outside France; they are still far from being definitive and abound in grave omissions and regrettable inclusions. But we have tried to give an idea of the main essentials of this aspect of Daumier as a painter which has been so strangely misunderstood although it might have seemed expressly designed for the largest of publics. It is enough for us to point out that the interest and novelty of this work consists above all in the assemblage of its illustrations, and it would not occur to me to attempt to make further additions to their silent eloquence. But it seems to me that from this conspectus of an artist's work the mind which lies behind it is revealed and gives us the opportunity of learning some valuable lessons ourselves.

Sketch.
(Claude Roger-Marx collection, Paris.)

DAUMIER THE MAN

One might easily say that the life of Daumier was uneventful; but how could one find a finer life-history than one which is merged in the production of a life-time's work? Our absurd curiosity will willingly expend itself upon tortured lives vainly consumed in the pursuit of unattainable ideas and achievements, lives whose romance but thinly conceals their emptiness. It is true that there is seldom a body of work of any importance in which one does not feel the presence of the man. But the man himself, we feel, must have subordinated all his ideals and ambitions to the perfection of a standard, a message, to bequeathe to posterity. Daumier is one of those who, with an unequalled whole-heartedness and generosity, put their all into their work.

The labour of erudition is not to be despised, but seldom does

Read of a Woman.
(Claude Roger-Marx collection, Paris.)

Mother and Child.
(Claude Roger-Marx collection, Paris.)

its task seem so thankless as in the case of Daumier, seldom so soon destined to mingle with the dust of events it attempts in vain to magnify. I shall forbear to describe the outward circumstances of a life whose eventfulness was wholly in the world of imagination. When we come to deal with the artist's work, in which difficulties of identification offer frequent problems, we shall find, I think, that even the most scientific historical researches can be of little use to us in what seems in this case almost a private matter. There are pictures which can be by Daumier; there are others which can equally not be by him.

It is perhaps time, too, that we reformed our conception of biography. It is not the salient facts which matter for the most part, it is all the tapestry of days which fill the canvas they weave. We shall find it but of feeble avail, with regard to the life of Daumier, to know that he was born in 1808 at Marseilles of a father who was a glazier and a poet and of a stalwart mother from the *midi*. The one event in a youth which had its difficulties but certainly also its illusions and its nobility was the arrival and establishment of the Daumier family in Paris. The child was to acquire an affection for the great city which was to end only with life. Eventually, across Daumier's first attempts at earning a living as a bailiff's errand boy and a bookseller's clerk, his vocation begins to assert itself, leading the way for him towards his real calling as a lithographer; but what mattered most in all this was the daily increasing contact he made with the popular life of the town, that spirit of Paris which was to awaken in revolt and with the lift of an elbow upset a whole *régime* while scarcely knowing what it had done. Already Daumier understood these stirrings and could follow them; but soon, with his first political works, he was to anticipate them by the interpretation of aspirations, of rebellious private opinions which the people themselves were still unable to formulate.

But this proud revolutionary period was not lasting. It was cut short by a trial, signalised even by a glorious condemnation to six months imprisonment; the law brought it to an end. For the future Daumier was to be the painter of life and manners, committed to the task of making the middle classes laugh at their own absurdities every morning of the year. But in this life of regular work, exacting, monotonous and without future, in this life of a day labourer, Daumier was making room for a real life, simple enough, one suspects, but, unless I am mistaken, a rich life too. Clearly we must resort to conjecture, but we have witnesses that are unmistakable in his work—work that in spite of restraint and fatigue develops unceasingly and has its own eloquence. It is impossible to conceive how much that work contains, how much and with what clarity and simplicity it tells us of the long meditations of a large-hearted man, his profound and personal reactions to the world and its ways—politics, business, and the life of the streets. There is no compromise, no base ambition, to disturb the outlook. But the man himself is moved to indignation by these things when they trouble other men, and, with the impassivity of good nature, he observes and he judges.

That imagination, the rectitude of that intellect, showed themselves more infallible than the most studied and best-reasoned discernment. How, but by that rare clairvoyance that strips an institution of its mark, could this minor journalist, after a few attendances in the remote press gallery at a few sittings of the Chamber of Deputies, have evoked so superbly and with such eternal verisimilitude « the vile body of the legislature »? How, unless he had been a man of that upright character that refuses to be deceived, could Daumier, from his memories as a bailiff's underclerk, from the recollection of two or three political trials, have amassed the evidence for that tremendous indictment of hypocrisy and meanness which is the burden of his work on themes of the Law Courts? By contrast, to render as he has done the poetry of the streets, the silhouettes of his labourers, his artisans and his idlers, the beauty of his landscapes with their varied hours, his nights, his dawns, his scenes of men at their work, a whole

Head of a Monk.
(Claude Roger-Marx collection, Paris.)

epic of daily life that none but he had yet observed, what qualities of vision Daumier must have had, how he must have lived in all he saw, with what largeness of heart he must have loved it all!

His simplicity, his good nature, his openness protected him from casual detractors. In the deepest recesses of his heart lay the storms of passion, the knowledge of all that is tragic in life, and the reserves of his indignation. But the world he created was such that he could dissipate his energies in no other. Daumier's outward life was admirably well-ordered. Sober, grave and silent, a generous friend and a family man (he married at the age of thirty-six and his whole life was lighted by this one simple affection), he gave rein to his humour only in his work; there, however, it expanded freely. A story told by the Goncourts under the date September 1853 has usually caused indignation among his biographers, but it gives us valuable evidence about Daumier's nature.

« Amusing remark made to Leroy by Daumier coming out from an evening with Boissard at the Hôtel Limodan in a state of slight intoxication: "How elderly I must be getting! In the old days I knocked my head against the stars, but now I couldn't even climb a lamp-post!" (*Ah, comme j'ai vieilli ! Autrefois les rues étaient trop étroites, je battais les deux murs... maintenant c'est à peine si j'accroche un volet !*) » And I think myself that when one is a Daumier, one is probably more often drunk with enthusiasm than with wine. Daumier's modesty probably concealed in the depths of his nature a great but well-justified self-confidence, that self-confidence which, for nature's gentlemen, is all-sufficing. I feel sure that with his indignations and his enthusiasms Daumier's life was a magnificent one, in spite of all his worldly embarrassments.

Let us examine his countenance as his contemporaries have handed it down to us, each in his own fashion, —the draughtsman, the sculptor, the writer and that sublime delineator of character, the photographer Nadar. It radiates an amazing warmth. « I admired his features », writes Théodore de Banville in his Memoirs, « they seemed to be bursting with strength and goodness. His eyes were small but piercing, his nose was turned up as though to sniff the breezes of the unknown. His mouth was well-cut, gracious and of large capacity. He had in fact a fine artist's head, very like that of some of the bourgeois he painted but burning with the bright flame of the spirit. »

« Daumier had rented a modest appartment in the Ile Saint-Louis, on the Quai d'Anjou. Over the top of it extended an enormous attic which in the eyes of the landlord was quite valueless. For in this once noble but now deserted neighbourhood space at that time counted for nothing. All the artist had to do was to have this attic plastered and open up a large window in the roof where there had been a sky-light to make himself a vast and splendid studio. This he had connected with his rooms by means of a frail and elegant spiral staircase. It is impossible to imagine any place less luxurious or more severely bare or from which ornaments had been more carefully excluded. On the walls, painted a soft light grey, there hung absolutely nothing except, perhaps, an unframed lithograph representing « The Pariahs » by Préault, the celebrated group refused by the jury of the exhibition in the days of the first battles for romanticism. There was a square black enamelled stove and some chairs. On the ground against the wall there were swollen portfolios overflowing with drawings and long since impossible to shut. And with the exception of the little table on which Daumier worked on his stones these were the entire contents of this large, light and cheerful studio. » This is almost word for word the same as the description the Goncourts, following Gavarni, give of Daumier's studio. « It was an enormous room in which, round a cast iron stove heated red hot, men were seated on the floor, each having within reach a bottle which he applied to his lips to drink, and in a corner a table covered with a heaped assorment of lithographic apparatus in appalling disorder, and in another corner a man, who was at the same time the artist's pupil and valet, cobbling and resoling some old shoes. »

To this very day a walk in the Ile Saint-Louis can easily be imagined as a pilgrimage in Daumier-land; at every turn one comes upon the setting, the whole climate and atmosphere of Daumier's works. Here are the evening idlers, here are the washerwoman's flight of steps and the irregular, romantic outlines of the little houses on the « Rive Gauche ». Daumier's own house is unchanged. Here is the staircase with its steps of bricks and mortar, and the studio, just as it was fifty years ago with a clear view over the roofs of the island as far as Notre-Dame; and the little side window that opens over the trees of the quayside, among the rustling leaves, into the landscapes that Daumier immortalised.

One last story will complete this sketch of Daumier's character. It is well known that at the end of the Second Empire the cross of the Legion of Honour was offered to Daumier and Courbet at the same time. Courbet ostentatiously rejected it while Daumier simply pleaded that he was too old. Albert Wolff in this connexion recounts that he happened to be at the house of

Sancho Panza.
(Claude Roger-Marx collection, Paris.)

Jules Dupré, the landscape painter, with Courbet « who could talk of nothing but the smack in the eye that he'd just given the Emperor ». He went with Courbet to the station of the Isle-Adam where they met Daumier. « At the sight of him a shout of joy burst from the depths of Courbet's enormous chest and flinging himself into the arms of his friend, he pressed him to his heart and exclaimed « Oh, how I love you! you've refused the cross like me, only you were quite wrong not to do it with more of a flourish! It was the sort of thing to make as much row as possible about ». Old Daumier shook his head and looking at Courbet from the depths of his eyes answered with a slight air of reproach « What would have been the good? I did what I thought was right and I am quite happy. It's nothing to do with the French Republic ». It is impossible to describe the exquisite dignity

Sketch for *The Thieves and the Ass*.
(Claude Roger-Marx collection, Paris.)

with which Daumier pronounced these words. His pride seemed to be revolted by the very thought that anyone could have supposed him capable of wanting to exploit his refusal as a means of advertisement. Courbet stood thunderstruck at this rebuke, and then as he got into the railway carriage with me he said to me « There's nothing to be done with Daumier; he's a regular visionary. »

All his life Daumier remained in the same way in the domain of eternal values. Two attitudes towards the events of life are possible for human beings: one is dictated by their interests which are often perfectly legitimate; the other takes the shapes suggested by their better nature. This latter attitude often surprises and even shocks their contemporaries, but it is soon seen to have a more lasting value. Frequently the source of improvidence, it is also the source of glory, while the other attitude soon passes into deserved oblivion. Daumier invariably chose the right gesture and made it without the slightest hesitation. The very lines of his face place him in that universal portrait-gallery of upright, simple men of wide vision who are for all time, and who for all other men are an infallible touchstone. One immediately recognises the lover of Daumier, just as one immediately recognises the lover of Bach.

**

But this fellow-feeling must be sought not in a figure of legend but in a profound knowledge of what Daumier really stood for. His name for a long time was a positive slogan, and it is to be feared that this was rather due to his political ideas than his artistic achievements. The sort of fame that did eventually come to him at the end of his life is therefore of but little importance. It was an idea, a principle personified by him that formed the real object of this veneration; that idea of the Republic which he had rendered in striking allegories during the struggle in opposition to Louis-Philippe, or the renascent Empire, as in the excitement of 1848. It was the very principle of democracy to which he gave life. But he personified these ideas at bottom only by virtue of his humanity and his creative power. It is in this aspect, a much livelier and richer one, that he most easily claims our affection.

« He was a Republican, » says Théodore de Banville, « spontaneously; it was the air he breathed. He was of the people and he loved the people from the bottom of his heart. » One must, I think, take

Sketch.
(Claude Roger-Marx collection, Paris.)

the words « Republican » and « people » in the widest sense. Under the Empire there was something fine about the Republic, and again under the Monarchy of July. If Republicanism is the dream of making one's country a better thing, a land of brothers unshackled by the useless apparatus of laws and regulations, a place where merit will be rewarded, justice and decency respected, then, under a government that is coarse, ignorant and inquisitorial, all the finer spirits are Republicans. But this sense of the word is as seldom understood under Governments that take the name of a Republic as under so-called Monarchies or Tyrannies. In reality this sort of Republicanism is entirely a moral attitude; it consists in having installed in oneself a new order of things and in that sense of justice to which in one's aspirations one appeals. To my way of thinking that is the only possible and the only valid revolution. It is certainly the only one which is consistent with itself, the only one that can stoop to no compromise, that can sacrifice nothing to make sure of its triumph in the world and in politics. The man who has once adopted such an attitude, even if he has no illusions about establishing his ideals in any earthly kingdom, never feels himself justified in yielding even for a moment to earthly temptations. On the contrary, he will feel his only justification to lie in the passionate assertion of the principles by which he lives himself. Daumier, honest atheist as he was, was nearer than he thought, in his purity of heart, to those who know that the Kingdom of God is not of this world, but for whom this knowledge is the best of all reasons for keeping the Kingdom of God in their heart.

Those who write about Daumier are frequently astonished by the furious violence of those attacks of his which come from the innermost depths of his being without the slightest restraint or mental reservation. One of these writers, Léon Rosenthal, who, in the narrower sense of the word is a good Republican, deprecates Daumier's ferocity about Louis-Philippe and the one-sidedness of his reproaches. Another, François Fosca, remarks with more insight that the real objects of Daumier's attacks are not individuals, but false moral principles and institutions. « The results seem savage but the artist was not. There was not an ounce of real hatred or cruelty in him. As one looks through the lithographs in which he lashes Louis-Philippe and his ministers, one clearly perceives that his victims were non-existent for him as human beings like himself and were merely colossal. Aunt-Sallies, tyrannical and grotesque Punch-and-Judies. » One notices, too, that in his cruellest satires, particularly in those which aim at social classes rather than individuals, the bourgeoisie, for instance, Daumier allows his feelings to be interpenetrated by a real pity for the victims he has deprived of all human semblance. But for Daumier with his simple and straightforward character, the supreme betrayal which affected him more than any other was that human beings should descend of their own accord to the status of bogeys and puppets. It is clear that he stigmatised it with a violence which the historian, accustomed to weigh pros and cons, will consider excessive. But one wonders whether Daumier was not right, whether it is not he who strikes the true note.

Politics and daily life have singularly cheapened the sense of the most sacred words —the Republic, Liberty, Peace and Fraternity are now nothing to us but vague entities impossible to retain in their entirety without compromise or weakness. But for Daumier it is different; these words again take on their most concrete interpretation and one feels that he personifies them without effort in those powerful allegories of his such as the workman who symbolises the liberty of the press in « Hands off! » or the figure of the Republic in « The Last Cabinet Meeting. »

The noble figure of the Republic which he calls into being in the Louvre picture has a force which is superhuman, that is to say, above history as written by mere men, and is at the same time a popular figure and a thing of flesh and blood. His inspiration is perhaps at its best in works which are not directly allegorical. Michelet perceived this when he wrote to him at the beginning of the Second Empire: « When you had the support of political inspiration, I used to be able to understand better your power of inexhaustible production. But at the present day you have not got this and yet you are just the same. You have well shown us that genius is a world in itself. I doubt whether you have ever done anything better than... that marvellously simple idea of the old people who beyond the ruins of demolition descry the sun. » And he goes on at the same time to reveal this beautiful symbol of the then existing situation. « And this sun, my dear Sir, when, I wonder, shall we see it again across the debris of this jerry-built structure which disfigures the face of France? What a consolation it is for you and me that nothing can age our country; that her original genius remains always young and strong!... Keep a firm hold on this marvellous spirit of youth of yours and on your gaiety of heart; they are signs of vigour. »

In fact Daumier's weapons, mockery anger and common-sense, are much the simplest and most effective; the scenes he evokes with their aid are much the most convincing. It is difficult not to smile at Rosenthal's indignation when he says that Daumier, while

Sketch.
(Claude Roger-Marx collection, Paris.)

calling himself a Republican and a Democrat (and, what is more, living as such) was at the same time « terrified by any idea of the transformation of society. » « And again he cast ridicule on aeronautics, railways and macadamised roads; he mocked at Pacifism and its apostles, Richard Cobden and Victor Hugo, he made fun of Socialism and made fairly serious accusations against Proud'hon and Victor Considérant. Above all he was the implacable foe of female emancipation! » But all these complaints only make us like Daumier even better, if that were possible; they come as a confirmation of his character as we have just drawn it. What better example could we find of his frankness and freedom? True to himself as always, Daumier here gives us the sane man's reactions. He does not hesitate to laugh at the absurdities of those who have been at times partisans of the same causes as himself. He rejects all clannishness of class or party, that clannishness of which Rosenthal is himself so striking an example and which is gradually reducing our age, consumed with deference even in its revolutions, to the silence which prevails in totalitarian countries. Daumier remains, as M. Jacques-Émile Blanche puts it, « a first-rate specimen of the Gallic race, irreverent and credulous, sceptical and inflammable and as hard on itself as on others. »

« It is the philosophy of a Pickwick (Le bonhomme Chrysale) » as Rosenthal cleverly remarks apropos of this attitude of Daumier's; but the remark, though amusing, does not carry conviction. To begin with, a Pickwick (le bonhomme Chrysale) of Daumier's temperament would not be nearly so absurd; and to go on with, I do not think that a conservative member of the middle classes from a romantic novel is a good analogy for Daumier. Here we have a man who is his own master, a self-made man who owes nothing to anyone, who reacts spontaneously to every event and loves or hates from his heart; a man who is alive and has an instinctive love of beauty and discovers it unerringly wherever it is; who has understood Paris, its people, and the life they live, better than any man has done to this day. And this man is hauled over the coals because he has no belief in hot air, because he is not interested in ideas which were never his, but which it is supposed that he ought to have had, because he knows nothing about foreign countries and because he laughs at progress.

Daumier, in fact, guided by an infallible instinct, goes straight to the heart of reality, and everything else is for him merely useless and tiresome convention. After fifty years, I wonder if any of us would care to defend against him any of the numerous discoveries he jeered at which have only contributed to the further enslavement of mankind? It would be better for us, I think, at this juncture if we remembered Baudelaire's observations. « You may take it, then, that in general human error does not affect my nerves except in so far as I care to extract the quintessence of stupidity for my own private satisfaction, as I have done during the last twenty years for *Le Siècle* (« This Age »). Apart from Chateaubriand, Balzac, Stendhal, Merimée, de Vigny, Flaubert, Banville, Gautier, Lecomte de Lisle, all the modern riffraff seem to me frightful. Your academicians—frightful—your liberals—equally frightful. Virtue and vice—both frightful—« art nouveau »—frightful. Progress—the most frightful of all. I hope I shall never again hear the words of these chatterboxes. The object of this volume of satire, « Belgium unveiled » (*La Belgique déshabillée*) is to mock at all that is usually called progress and which I call the heathenism of idiots. » There is little to add to this blood-stained apostrophe, bloodstained because Baudelaire paid for his knowledge with his blood and had the right to say what he liked. But what a fascinating encounter this is between the two great spirits who dominate the nineteenth century. They form a fraternal pair of the greatest dignity, one being the most aristocratic spirit in our literature, the other representing the most genuinely popular element in the history of our arts... This approximation of Daumier to Baudelaire owes nothing to chance. It would be possible to place many of their paintings and poems side by side and find in each the same sentiments, for instance in the matter of their mutual comprehension of Paris; but the two men also knew, understood, and admired each other. As in the case of Constantin Guys, it is impossible to think of Daumier without remembering those pages, so remarkably prophetic, which Baudelaire consecrated to him. As early as 1860 Baudelaire had written for a newspaper a critical essay composed under the influence of an unlimited admiration for Daumier. At this time the artist was considered dangerously subversive. The author was compelled to withdraw his article with this explanation: « As you think that my article is impossible to publish under the regime of Napoleon III. and Walewski the First, it must simply be suppressed, » he wrote to Louis Martinet: « I have a sincere regard for you but I cannot submit to circumstances. It has been my habit since childhood to believe that I am invariably right... Your belief is wrong; it is the result of a foolish timidity, and I am convinced that the article, if it appeared, would give pleasure to everyone. »

Head.
(Photo Druet.)

In 1868 there appeared, in the volume entitled *Aesthetic Curiosities*, in the chapter devoted to various French caricaturists, the long study which begins with these words:

« I am going to speak of one of the most important men, I will not say merely in caricature but in modern art, a man who amuses the population of Paris every morning and daily satisfies the need for public gaiety by giving it something to feed on. The bourgeois, the businessman, the street-boy and the house-wife often laugh and pass on, ungrateful creatures, without noticing the artist's name. Up to now only artists have grasped that there is something serious about him, something that would really supply material for a treatise. As you may guess, it is about Daumier... » There follows a detailed analysis of the most striking phases of Daumier's work in lithography from the attacks on Louis-

Two Lawyers.
(Claude Roger-Marx collection, Paris.)

Philippe to the Robert Macaire series, a general satire on Parisians, a caricature which has entered the domain of the novel and of ancient history « blaspheme who will its utility. »

« As far as morals are concerned, Daumier has several affinities with Molière; like him, he goes straight to the point; the idea is at once apparent, one looks and one sees at once. The legends inscribed below the drawings are not of much use, they could usually be dispensed with. His fun is, so to speak, involuntary; the artist does not need to look for his ideas, one might almost say they escaped from him without his knowing. His caricatures are alarmingly broad but without rancour or spite. There is a basis of honesty and good nature in all his work. He often refused—it is a trait that calls for notice—to use certain admirable but violent motives for satire because, he said, they exceeded the limits of the comic and might have wounded the conscience of humanity. So whether he is horrifying or terrible, it is almost unintentionally. He put down what he saw and that was the result. As he has a passionate love of nature, he rarely rises to the absolute in absurdity. He even avoids with care everything that might not be the object of immediate and clear perception for a public of Frenchmen. What completes the remarkable character of Daumier and gives him a special rank in the illustrious family of artists, is that his drawing is naturally coloured; his lithographs evoke ideas of colour; there is something else in his pencil beside the black which is necessary to outline the contours; one guesses his colour as one guesses a writer's thoughts. It is the sign of an uncommon talent and all intelligent artists have clearly perceived it in his work. »

What one gathers from these conclusions is the almost prophetic way in which Baudelaire understands the sense of Daumier's works in their entirety when he practically only knew his lithographs. He has already discovered the promise of magnificent work in colour, the fulfilled proof of unity of thought. He attempts to place him in his period in his right position, far above that which was commonly assigned to him.

It would be impossible to over-emphasize the importance of this assignment of place. It served to prove once more that there is no such thing as a misunderstood genius. Even in the case of those men whom the Gods have chastised most severely and who are most disquieting to their fellowmen, one discovers certain privileged beings who have understood them and whose witness is enough for posterity. It is enough that a Van Gogh or a Cézanne should have had ten friends, ten just men, in order that their century should be saved. The great thing, if one lives in their century, is to be one of those ten.

It is no mere chance that Daumier was so long misunderstood as a painter; he had succeeded with his lithographs to the point of satiety—a moral success at least, for lack of a material one. For decades it had been his profession to make Paris laugh and think. His thousands of plates were spread throughout the Press and the newsagents had carried his name into the depths of the most inaccessible of middle-class houses. These plates for half a century had been the most faithful commentary on the history of France. But we are dealing with his painted work, with the attainment of universality. No one will at first find himself particularly attracted or held by the generalised style which prevails in this work, but everyone will be compelled to recognise himself in it. In an art divested of all transitory elements and all contemporary appeal, Daumier was to enshrine for posterity his whole experience of humanity.

All this was above the heads of the mass of his contemporaries, and Daumier showed little anxiety to enlighten them. But the noblest and best men of his time knew and loved him. Delacroix, who took the trouble to copy his compositions; Baudelaire, whose art is so often strangely allied; Balzac, and Michelet, who dreamed of composing his captions, and Corot, who helped him in his sad old age with infinite tact and deference. The esteem of these few men was well worth that of a larger public. The exhibition of his work in 1878 organised by his friends, though it was not a popular success, was none the less to consecrate in the eyes of all the true elite the great painter who was then passing away.

DAUMIER'S ACHIEVEMENT

From a general point of view, what is surprising in Daumier's work is that it forms no chapter in the history of the development of our arts. We know nothing of the formation of the artist's style except that as a child he no doubt frequented the Louvre and drew from the antique. He had never travelled, though one feels that he had understood and assimilated the Flemish and Italian schools. Of his tastes and preferences we know nothing. He had no master even in the acquirement of the technique of his art. He had scarcely made his first appearance as a political caricaturist when it was clear that he was already a master. From the first he had the sense of the setting of a page and of proportions. He had above all an almost sculptural gift for volume. This gift showed itself in the habit he had of modelling little statuettes in terracotta while the memory of his victims was still fresh in his mind and using them afterwards as models for his lithographs. This was the way he did his gallery of political portraits and their synthesis, « the vile body of the legislature. » The most

Street Scene.
(Claude Roger-Marx collection, Paris).

celebrated plates, *Rue Transnonain, Enfoncé Lafayette* (« Lafayette in the soup »), are youthful works. When one considers the work of the best-known artists of the time, such as Raffet, Charlet, Grandville and Monnier, one can see how dazzling a revelation was the appearance of Daumier and how formidable an antagonist he must have looked. A few years later, being prevented from continuing his work on political themes, he created with the same facility a new line, the caricature of manners and customs. Finally, last of all, when fashion had changed and passed him by, he again discovered a style of extreme trenchancy to stigmatise the feebleness of the dying Empire and the horrors of war and defeat. It has often been said that in his last lithographic productions Daumier, in his weary old age, was unable to avoid repetition and a slackening of tension in line. This is entirely wrong. The fact is, these works were reproduced under the most unfavourable conditions with a negligence and a contempt for what was due to the artist that are unforgivable. But to the very last, Daumier never ceased to intensify the delicacy and suppleness of his drawing; to broaden his style, and to express more with less means. This was, of course, too, the time when he was at last able to devote himself to oil-painting and drawing and we already know to what summits of triumphant expression he attained in these domains.

It is generally thought that Daumier began painting in oils towards the end of the July monarchy, but it was particularly from 1860 onwards that he found the leisure (enforced leisure, since work was more and more difficult for him to find) to devote himself entirely to his art. His painting is even more surprising than his lithography, and far more difficult to place in its true historical perspective. Daumier painted in the second half of the nineteenth century in the interval between the triumph of Corot and the Barbizon School and the foundation of impressionism. He showed himself entirely uninfluenced by the new trends. He has been called the last and the only romantic artist, and it is true that having formed his style about 1830 and having at once attained the most complete mastery, his conception of painting must date from that time. But he never put it into practice until twenty years later, and this dislocation possibly explains the isolation of Daumier among his contem-

The Walk.
(Claude Roger-Marx collection, Paris.)

Sketch.
(Claude Roger-Marx collection, Paris.

poraries; and the truth is that though it is possible to call Daumier the only truly romantic artist, it would be unjust to connect him with the style of 1830. His romanticism is much deeper and more real and individual; he opens a new chapter in French art.

It would be interesting one day to write a history of Romanticism, not emphasizing its point of departure but the way it was worked out; one could leave out the anecdotes and the more theatrical manifestations, whose only objects were to arouse contemporary astonishment, and concentrate on genuine innovations. It might emerge from such an inquiry that the peak of Romanticism and its culmination is the moment at which it had succeeded in adapting a traditional style to the expression of new ideas, the moment at which it rejoins Classicism, which it then passes and prolongs. A positive contribution of this sort could certainly not have been the product of the school of 1830 with its antiquarianism, its artifice and its rhetoric. It was more likely to have come, in the years that followed, from these first delineators of the modern world, Balzac, Baudelaire and Daumier. In them Romanticism took shape and found a real justification for its existence. It is Baudelaire and not de Musset who portray the nineteenth century physically and morally, and who expresses the anguish and the crisis of mystical feeling in the face of the growth of materialism. It is Baudelaire who has created the current of modern French poetry, personal, subjective and without superannuated didactic apparatus. It is Daumier and not Victor Hugo who has shown without artifice the abyss of human contradictions—the drama of institutions in opposition to individuals, the struggle of the private conscience against unfair environment. It is Daumier who has told of the power of modern man as well as his suffering, a power which is a kind of faith; he is the first to express the heroism of modernity. It is an astonishing coincidence that we find Daumier fulfilling the prophecy in the note Delacroix wrote in his journal (1824) entitled « on the men of this time: Michaelangelo and Goya. »

We have said that this work in oils owed its great freedom of expression to the fact that it followed upon the already well-developed lithographic work. Daumier's painting seems to stand above Time, above the accidents of events and without connexion with the exterior world. Having thus reached a convention that is entirely classic, it is accessible to every age. It nevertheless profoundly expresses its period even in its most concrete details. Undoubtedly the best way for an artist to attain universality is to find it in his immediate surroundings. The opposition between so-called realist painters who would seek to transfer reality all alive into their canvas and others who prefer to resort to symbols to express their feelings, is a meaningless contrast. The truth is that realism is ineffective and meaningless unless it discovers, behind the features or the actions which it reproduces, the motives which animate them; and symbolism is mere empty decoration and idle convention unless beneath an indirect presentation it conceals a deep feeling of ever-present reality, eager for outlet. Observation must not rest content with the superficial or imagination with the merely gratuitous.

In the case of Daumier, he obviously both managed allegory with conscious thought and reproduced reality with intuitive insight. As a painter of reality, he gives reality the value of myth; as a symbolist, he chooses his symbols with a profound regard for actuality. We have noticed that he often treated the same themes in his paintings as in his lithographs, but in his paintings, since they were not designed for readers eager for sensation, Daumier divests his subjects of all their elements of caricature and forced grimace. It is clearly a natural tendency with him because it frequently appears, even when he felt himself more free to do as he liked in his lithographic work. In many of his plates, the comic disappears altogether and the draughtsman finally prevails over the caricaturist. In others one feels a positive predilection for ugliness. An attempt has been made to deduce from this that Daumier had a sort of cult for the horrible and the monstrous, and because he excelled in depicting aged horrors, procuresses, vinegary landladies, divorce-mongers and blue-stockings, the claim has been made in particular that he never shows women except in their most absurd and degraded aspects. No doubt in his lithographs he was under the spell of the obscure dictates of comic journalism, and this must not be forgotten, for in his paintings no similar bias is discernible; there woman is never conceived in an unpleasant guise. We find in them most often the ponderous silhouette of the hard-working but healthy woman of the people, the washerwoman, the laundress and the factory girl; but we also find the fresh, surprised face of the young girl in *La Confidence*,

Clown. Drawing accentuated with water-colours.
(Claude Roger-Marx collection, Paris.)

and some charming scenes of motherhood, as well as children at play. One of these faces alone is enough to outweigh thousands of the female monstrosities, the hideous lawyers or timorous citizens, and to prove that Daumier was susceptible to beauty.

And what is more, this new type which he created of the prolific working-woman is a particularly moving tribute to the beauty of human functions. It is a beauty which surpasses in its strange mobility the loveliness which belongs merely to the domain of charm and of pleasure. Daumier thus strikes out a new and audacious line and enriches our conception of the beautiful. How can he be judged by recognised standards? Beauty is unforeseen and changeable; it has only to be incarnated anew once again in the peculiar vision of a man of genius for us to discover a new and surprising aspect of it.

Daumier, romantic as he was, has expressed the reality of modern life. The figures in his lithographs reproduce particular moments of living history; the figures in his painted work abandon the anecdotic and have a generic value, the expression of true universality beneath the mask of the temporal. In their creation Daumier had recourse to the powers he had acquired by the long practice of his craft, the rejection of useless detail, the gift of quick observation and hard hitting. The backgrounds of his pictures as of his lithographs are bare, precise and suggestive. He lays bare the bones of the landscape, as François Fosca says, as he does with those figures which he first composed in the nude or even constructed from the skeleton. In the eyes of Daumier, the world is stripped of all its façades; he shows it as it is, and we too, as we cast our eyes over his work, see it as he does.

In one chapter of his work, Daumier shows a peculiar greatness; in his scenes of Paris and her realities. In thousands of his lithographs he has shown picturesque or amusing details of city life, but in some of his paintings he seems to concentrate the soul of the city, its very breath of life as well as its features. In the icy morning hour the washerwoman comes up from the Seine, a bundle of linen under her arm; women, whose sagging forms tell of hard work, stand out in dark, laborious silhouette against the white buildings of the quay. One thinks of Baudelaire's lines in the *Tableaux Parisiens* which so often seem like a marginal comment on one whole side of Daumier's work.

> Dawn in her green-coloured and rosy garment quakes;
> Over the lonely Seine there slowly creeps the sun,
> And in the half-light Paris rubs her eyes, and takes
> Her working-things in hand like some old charwoman.
>
> *L'aurore grelottante en robe rose et verte*
> *S'avançait lentement sur la Seine déserte*
> *Et le sombre Paris en se frottant les yeux*
> *Empoignait ses outils, vieillard laborieux.*

And then there is the *Water Carrier*, the *Blacksmith* and the *Woodcutter*, those obscure celebrants of some strange and solemn rite. And here too in:

> The interlaced byways of ancient capitals
> Where all things, even horror, turn to sorcery.
> *Dans les plis sinueux des vieilles capitales,*
> *Où tout même l'horreur tourne aux enchantements.*

are the triumphant processions of scavengers, the trembling grace of bathers, and the loungers in the fraternal amity of their evening walk...

> City of busy crowds, city of endless dreams.
> *Fourmillante cité, cité pleine de rêves.*

The Print Collectors stand in the afternoon sunlight; the imagination already begins to stir:—

> To any child in love with atlases and prints
> The earth appears too small for his vast appetite.
> *Pour l'enfant amoureux de cartes et d'estampes,*
> *L'univers est égal à son vaste appétit.*

Daumier has no need to have recourse to allegory to retain a universal form of expression; he makes of a humble street-scene a thing of myth. But he leaves it all its human value; he never falls into the horrors of abstraction or the redundant verbiage of romanticism. As he works out the dramatic series of the « Mountebanks » (*Les Saltimbanques*), all he is doing is to illustrate that well-worn theme of conflicting emotion, the clown who laughs through his tears, the sad heart beneath the tinsel of the fair. Victor Hugo had already drawn from this theme the last effects of unintentional absurdity; with Daumier it remains moving and true. It is because, in his recourse to allegory, he is merely seeking a more powerful expressiveness, and ceaselessly adds to it both what he has observed in external appearances in others and also what he has gathered from his own experience.

Daumier went straight for the greatest of all modern literary myths, Don Quixote, and he went for it perfectly simply and calmly, without deliberation or false shame; and, to the universal surprise, he proved himself up to it. That was the genesis of that sublime reincarnation, the only one, I think, which is not merely literary, of great literature in art. Artists have been inspired by other characters in fiction, Hamlet and Faust for instance. There have been various interpretations. But none of them have come to life, to carnal palpitating life, more vivid than if it had had real existence, as Don

Quixote has in the hands of Daumier. Daumier seems to take part in those jousts himself; as though by some strange doubling of personality he is Sancho wringing his hands in despair, he is Don Quixote charging the windmills; the prudent traditionalist and the cavalier of the ideal; the madman in whose madness there is reason and the sane man yet the madder for following him. Magnificent illustrations for Cervantes' masterpiece could be made from all the drawings and all the paintings it inspired from Daumier. There are no other figures in them beside these two immortals, but their wild and monotonous cavalcade lives again in them with gripping power. « Standing up above the horizon » writes Élie Faure, « they seem so tall that one recoils at their approach; the idealist and the materialist marching together, figures older and more lasting than the universe itself. Though he knew not Spain, Daumier has evoked it with superhuman, almost surrealist reality. His figures live amid the aridity and devastation which makes the scenery of that land the counterpart of a spiritual creation. It is amazing that this man in his simplicity should have been able so to steep himself in the heart of that masterpiece of literature, and enrich it in his turn. And he has done it by his astounding faculty for living it over again with the honesty and good will he brought to all he did. It is usually the author who is taken by his own snare and treads deep in the footsteps of the creatures he has made. So has Cervantes done and his myriads of readers after him. And Daumier, too, has followed. But he alone had power to blaze the trail of that once-more-ridden ride with the sign-manual of immortality. »

Daumier was not less familiar with the conventions of the stage. Here, too, he accosts the greatest figures and makes them part of his personal universe. He calls up the *Malade Imaginaire* with hallucinatory powers of evocation and the man at grips with the agonies of his pitiable nature is truer than truth itself. It has been asked whether Daumier could or could not be described as cultivated. Certainly there is nothing about him that reminds us of the study or of the discipline of scholarship. But everything goes to prove that he had what is better than book-learning, a natural familiarity with masterpieces. By the way he enters into the creation of Don Quixote or the characters of Molière one recognises his power of going straight to the essence of things in his approach to the sublime. Here as ever, Daumier's instinct did not deceive him. He had the advantage over cultivated men, in the ordinary sense of the word, which is possessed by those natural beings who have enough simplicity of heart and spontaneity to live through a literary creation perfectly concretely and to believe in it absolutely. Only, just at those points where the vulgar herd are loud in their applause of melodrama and bombast, Daumier goes straight for the truth. We have probably too far forgotten his literary inheritance from his father, a worthy artisan with a

Workmen.
(Claude Roger-Marx collection, Paris.)

25

touching ambition for culture. Daumier probably found at home much of that encumbrance of standard works with which the self-taught blithely surround themselves. Among these he chose by instinct the finest and got to know them well, partly by mere contact and partly by the correspondences with them which he found within himself; thus in a simple way he came to understand them. Apart from those evocations of an antiquity he revered and whose modern travesties he pitilessly denounced, he is known to have wanted to illustrate the Iliad and the Odyssey or at least Fénelon's *Télémaque*. Baudelaire had the same ideas for him. In 1860 he wrote to Poulet-Malassis, recommending Daumier, who had just been turned off the Charivari, and was now free and with no occupation but painting. « Think of the Pharsalia and Aristophanes; those two ideas date from fifteen years ago. This is a good and splendid thing. » It is indeed impossible to think without emotion of what it meant for Baudelaire to choose Daumier as early as 1846 to illustrate the great poem of Latinity on the eve of its decline, that Pharsalia which, he says « is always so sparkling in its melancholy, so heart-rending in its stoicism. » (Letter to Sainte-Beuve in 1866.)

Thus whether he is describing the world or expressing it in symbols, Daumier always puts himself, his own nature, in the centre of his creative work. The imperfections of his work in oils may perhaps shock a period like ours which is accustomed to subtleties of technique and to the Byzantinism of art for art's sake. But all this is powerless to make us forget or misconceive Daumier's will to expression. Painting is for him a language, and in this sense it is possible to say that his thought passed far beyond the limits of the frame he himself gave it. One felt this in practice at the exhibition at the *Orangerie* in 1934. The high walls of the room have never seemed so richly filled as by those few paintings of such comparatively modest physical proportions. One can see the same thing in the reproductions of these paintings; they have a breadth, a monumental effect which is unmistakable, for Daumier has conferred on them not merely the image of some earthly scene, but also something of his own intimate conception. His method of production undoubtedly influenced this side of his work. It is not unimportant to know that he always drew from memory. An old controversy has arisen in this connexion between the partisans of drawing from Nature and the partisans of memory-drawing. In reality, the defects of which the latter method is accused come from a confusion between it and slickness or *chic*. That, of course, does tend to develop into mere mannerism or cliché; drawing from memory, on the other hand, by separating a work of representation into two stages, facilitates both the conscious and the unconscious methods of creation, and gives the artist's mind the time to itemise and classify its sensations; the transposition necessary in a work of art is thus undoubtedly facilitated. We may note besides that Ingres, the champion of drawing from Nature, never hesitated, if it suited his personal vision better, to alter Nature, for instance by adding several extra vertebrae to the spine of an *odalisque*. Delacroix, Daumier and, in our own time, Rodin all drew from memory; their respective works certainly gained from that fact in liberty and interior logic. « The living model never answers well to the idea or impression that the painter wishes to express, » said Delacroix, « one must therefore learn to do without one, and for that one must acquire facility, furnish one's memory to the point of infinitude, and make numerous drawings after the old masters. »

Baudelaire, too, defended memory-drawing from his own point of view. « In fact, » he wrote in *L'Art Romantique*, « all actual good draughtsmen draw from the image inscribed in their brain and not direct from Nature... When a real artist comes to the point of the final execution of his work, the model will be more hindrance than help to him. It even happens that men like Daumier and M. G. (Constantin Guys) who have long been accustomed to exercise their memory and to fill it with images, find their prime faculty troubled and as it were paralysed before the multiplicity of details which the presence of a model involves. » (This is confirmed by two anecdotes reported by M. Raymond Escholier. Daumier, when he wanted to make a portrait of Henri Monnier, did it before the agreed time for the sitting had elapsed; but another day when he wanted to get a drawing of some ducks, he refused the sketch-book and pencil which were offered him and simply looked at them, explaining that he was unable to draw from Nature.) Baudelaire pushes his thought to curious conclusions. « A duel therefore begins between the wish to see everything and forget nothing, and the faculty of memory, which has the habit of vividly absorbing the general colour, the silhouette and the arabesque of the outline. An artist who has a perfect sense of form, but has the habit of exercising above all his memory and imagination, finds himself, therefore, assaulted, as it were, by a mob of details all demanding justice with the fury of a crowd of enthusiasts for absolute equality of rights. All justice is then necessarily violated, all harmony destroyed and sacrificed; this or that triviality usurps enormous proportions. The more the artist relies impartially on detail, the more the anarchy increases. » Impressionism at the same moment was establishing itself on a basis of fidelity to Nature, even in her most fickle subtleties. One wonders whether Baudelaire was not giving in advance the true reasons for the check in this movement, at least in so far as affected its position as a school.

Daumier, on the other hand, by the exercise of his prodigious memory, retains full mastery and control over the details he summons to aid him in his work. « What distinguishes him is his certainty, » Baudelaire again says, « he draws like the great masters, his drawing is abundant and facile, it is an improvisation pressed to its conclusions... He has a marvellous and almost divine memory which serves him instead of a model. His figures are always well drawn, always true in movement. His talent of observation is so accurate that one never finds a single head which does not fit the body that supports it; the right nose, the right forehead, an eye like that, this sort of foot and that hand; it is the logic of a scientist transferred into an art so light, so fugitive, that it has the very mobility of life itself. » The drawings and sketches of Daumier are particularly instructive in this connexion. As M. Claude Roger Marx, who knows them particularly well, observes « one likes them not because one is a slave to the present fashionable perversity of preferring the detail to the whole or the sketch to the finished work, but on the contrary because each one constitutes a perfect work of art in itself. » They escape the confines of all criticism and all comparison; in them Daumier's thought is expressed with that superhuman freedom which belongs only to the very great. Those horses, those portraits which loom up from a few thickly-clustered strokes can be put side by side with the drawings of Rembrandt. « An inexplicable logic, » writes M. Claude Roger Marx, « imposes order upon these indications which at first seem so chaotic; from all these confused and contradictory strokes there emerges a marvellous unity. The charcoal chequers the page with broad areas of light; the pen and the pencil have a certainty, a sharpness and a delicacy that are exquisite. Here the touch is light, equal and refined; there it is rich and thick, of the consistency of the black of a lithograph. Here the masses are defined by enveloping curves and concentric circles; there by outlines that are perpetually broken. Here the play of light and shade is emphasised by the grain of the *crayon*; here by slashes of ink or wash, which give the white a glowing value. »

But the foundation of all Daumier's work, his drawing, remains the architecture of his methods of thought. His gifts of execution are never exercised to represent the features of a natural model merely mechanically; its

The Riot.
(Claude Roger-Marx collection, Paris).

Sketch.
(Claude Roger-Marx collection, Paris).

power is used, on the contrary, to interpret every caprice of an imagination eager to create life. I doubt if one finds in any other artist so complete a subservience of the hand to the mind that guides it. Even in its most sublime intoxications, even in its maddest moments, Daumier's genius retains its full consciousness.

DAUMIER TODAY

Daumier's truth to life has been proclaimed by everyone, and to be convinced of it it is only necessary to trust appearances in their most obvious forms. One of these is the anecdote of Gambetta, surprised at thinking he could recognise in a painting certain famous lawyers whom the artist had certainly never known. Relating the story in his preface to the 1934 Exhibition, M. de Monzie adds that we may well feel again 56 years later the surprise which Gambetta felt. There is according to him a certain permanence in professional traditions and in human functions, which once seized in a work of art in its typical forms remains for ever expressive. I prefer to think, however, that it is really fashions, habits and peculiarities which change while men remain the same. If one considers them closely, the lawyers of the present day, in spite of the analogy of costume, have different attitudes from those one sees in Daumier's lawyers. There is nevertheless an underlying resemblance; for the fact is, that beneath all physical changes, human character does not change. It is a thing which once seized and noted down in a work of art will give that work eternal value.

In the same way, it would be quite easy to illustrate a modern paper with Daumier's satires. Our *bourgeois* are as timid, ignorant, vain and touching as ever; our crooks are just as numerous, just as coarse and just as happy. But our race has also preserved, with all its faults and failings, the same contact with reality in the eternal gestures of every craft and calling. It has kept its national feelings and its national virtues. The atmosphere which surrounds it, the frame within which its life passes, the city which is its incarnation, are unchanged despite every mutilation. The embodiment which Daumier has given them will perhaps one, day when they have disappeared, ensure them a continued life.

One cannot but recognies that a new miracle must necessarily occur every time that an artist, devoted to representing in plastic form the images of things, is able to translate in that guise their most secret significance. Daumier possessed this gift of divination in its highest form, that is, he possessed it naturally. Classicism had taken refuge in a land of myth, in order to raise the permanent conflicts of life above the level of daily birth and death. But why resort to allegory when every day brings a fresh symbol? Daumier, who had the power of reanimating conventions, had also the power of investing his own time and the men of his own time with the epic quality which is that of real life. So, thanks to him, his age lives again for us, with its full value and its full intimacy, without our having to wait for a future transposition in the long labours of legend and of mythology. This implies peculiar and difficult conditions for his work; it can never dispense with a certain necessary dignity. We wholly misunderstand its beauty and its scope if we are surprised that it did not give fuller expression to that smiling and easy aspect of the beauty of creation which most romantic artists have emphasized. But its dignity will only make it more simple and more familiar to us.

Probably this heroic tone in treating of daily life will seem rather surprising to an epoch desiccated by irony and fed on fine phrases. Daumier in the least of his works has a breath of the eternal which to fools is alarming. Clear proof, this, that men being divided into two classes, the superior sort and the others, the former, to whatever class, epoch or race they belong, are at bottom one family —how far alas! above the crowd!

Daumier is as alive today as ever. Nothing in his work has staled. There is nothing to add to it. In its affirmation of the permanence of man and his mission it is far more eloquent and more straight-forward than all the theorists and essayists of our day. Its purpose is to give full illustration and expression to the two words which perhaps for the very reason that they are the most beautiful are, in his century as in ours, the most abused, the words « Real » and « Ideal. »

BIBLIOGRAPHY

BOOKS

BAUDELAIRE (Charles). — L'Art romantique. Paris, Michel Lévy, 1868, in-18.
BAUDELAIRE (Charles). — Curiosités esthétiques. Paris, Michel Lévy, 1866, in-18.
GONCOURT (E. and J. de). — Gavarni. Paris, Plon, 1873, in-8.
CHAMPFLEURY. — Histoire de la caricature moderne. Paris, Dentu, 1878, in-18.
CHAMPFLEURY. — Essai de catalogue de l'œuvre lithographiée. Paris, Librairie Parisienne, 1878, in-8°.
CATALOGUE of the exhibition of paintings and drawings by Honoré Daumier. Foreword by Champfleury. Paris, Gauthier-Villars, 1878, in-18.
CHESNEAU (Ernest). — Peintres et statuaires romantiques. Paris, Charavay Frères, 1880, in-18.
GONCOURT (E. and J. de). — La maison d'un artiste. Paris, G. Charpentier, 1881, 2 volumes in-18.
BANVILLE (Th. de). — Petites Études. *Mes Souvenirs.* Paris, G. Charpentier, 1882, in-12.
CLARETIE (Jules). — Honoré Daumier, 1810-1879. Paris, Librairie des Bibliophiles, 1882.
GRIGOUX (Jean). — Causeries sur les artistes de mon temps. Paris, Calmann-Lévy, 1885.
BERALDI (H.). — Les graveurs du XIXe siècle. Paris, L. Conquet, 1885-1892, 12 volumes in-8°.
GONCOURT (E. and J. de). — *Journal.* Paris, Charpentier et Fasquelle, 1887-1896, 9 volumes in-12.
ALEXANDRE (Arsène). — Honoré Daumier : l'homme et l'œuvre. Paris, H. Laurens, 1888, in-4°.
COQUIOT (Gustave). — H. Daumier, 1808-1879. Paris, Larousse, 1901.
MARX (Roger). — Étude sur l'école française, Paris (*La Gazette des Beaux-Arts*, 1903).
HAZARD (N. A.) and DELTHEIL (Loys). — Catalogue raisonné de l'œuvre lithographique de Honoré Daumier. Orruy, N. A. Hazard, 1904, large in-8°.
FRANTZ (Henri) and UZANNE (Octave). — Daumier et Gavarni. Special number of « The Studio », London, 1904, in-4°.
MEIER GRAEFE (Julius). — Entwickelungsgeschichte der modernen Kunst. Stuttgart, 1904.
MARCEL (Henry). — Honoré Daumier. Paris, 1906, in-8°.
BAUDELAIRE (Charles). — Correspondance. Paris (*Mercure de France*, 1907).
CARY (Elizabeth Luther). — Honoré Daumier, together with an introductory essay on his art. New-York, G. P. Putnam's Sons, 1907, in-4°.
ILLUSTRATED CATALOGUE of the Exhibition of the works of H. Daumier at the Galerie L. et P. Rosenberg et Fils, Paris, 1907.
BERTELS (Kurt). — Honoré Daumier als lithograph. Munich and Leipzig, R. Piper, 1908, in-4°.
KLOSSOWSKI (Erich). — Honoré Daumier. Munich, R. Piper, 1908, in-4°, new edition in 1923.
ROSENTHAL (Léon). — Honoré Daumier. Paris, « L'art de notre temps », collection, 1912.
ROSENTHAL (Léon). — Du romantisme au réalisme. Paris, H. Laurens, 1914, in-8°.
CATALOGUE of the retrospective exhibition of the works of Honoré Daumier. Liége, 1914.
PENNELL (Joseph) and ROBINS PENNELL (E.). — Lithography and Lithographers. London, 1915.
HAUSENSTEIN (W.). — Daumier zeichnungen. Munich, 1918.
WALDMANN (Emil). — Honoré Daumier. Recht und Gericht. Berlin, 1919.
RUMANN (Arthur). — Daumier als Illustrator. Daumier der Meister der Karikatur. 2 vols., Munich, 1919 and 1920.
CATALOGUE of Lithographs by Honoré Daumier on sale at the Hôtel Drouot, Paris, 1920.
FUCHS (Eduard). — Werke Honoré Daumier. I Holzschnitte : 1833-1870 ; II Lithographien : 1828-1851 ; III Lithographien : 1852-1860 ; IV Lithographien : 1861-1872. Munich, Albert Langen, 1922, 4 vols. small in-folio.
ESCHOLIER (Raymond). — Daumier, peintre et lithographe. Paris, Floury, « La vie et l'art romantiques », 1923, in-4°.
FONTAINAS (André). — La peinture de Daumier. Paris, Crès, « Ars Graphica », Études et documents, n° 1, 1923, in-4°.
GAUFFIN (A.). — Corot, Daumier, Guys. Stockholm, 1923.
REY (Robert). — Daumier. Paris, Stock, « Les Contemporains », 1923, in-32.
WALDMANN (Emil). — Honoré Daumier. Leipzig, E. A. Seemann, 1923.
MARTINE (Charles) and MAROTTE (Léon). — Dessins de maîtres français. IV Honoré Daumier. 50 drawings printed in several shades, with a study and a catalogue. Paris, Helleu et Sergent, 1924.
BAUDELAIRE (Charles). — Les dessins de Daumier. Paris, Crès, « Ars Graphica », Études et documents, n° 2, 1924, in-4°.
SADLER (Michael). — Daumier, the Man and the Artist. London, Halton and Smith, 1924.
SERVIAN (Ferdinand). — Remarques sur la technique de quelques peintres provençaux, J.-A. Constantin, Granet, H. Daumier, Monticelli, Ricard, Marseille, Barlatier, 1924, in-8°.
ROTHE (Hans). — Daumier und die Politik. — Daumier und das Theater. — Daumier und die Ehe. — Daumier und die Justiz. 4 vols., Leipzig, List, 1924-1928.
FAURE (Élie). — Histoire de l'art. Vol. IV. Paris, Crès, 1926, in-8°.
FELS (Florent). — Les Cent Robert Macaire d'H. Daumier. Paris, Les Arts et le livre, 1926.
RUMANN (Arthur). — Honoré Daumier. Berlin, 1926.
DELTHEIL (Loys). — Le peintre graveur illustré. Vols. XX to XXIX bis : Daumier. Paris, 1926-1930, 9 volumes, in-folio.
FONTAINAS (André). — Daumier. Album d'art Druet. Paris, Librairie de France, 1927.
FUCHS (Eduard). — Der Maler Daumier. Munich, Albert Langen, 1927, small in-folio.
CATALOGUE of the sale of the Paul Bureau collection at the Galerie Georges Petit, Paris, 1927.
CATALOGO della II Esposizione Internazionale dell' Incisione moderna. Florence, 1927.
ALEXANDRE (Arsène). — Daumier. Paris, Rieder, « Maîtres de l'art moderne », 1928, in-8°.
FOCILLON (Henri). — La peinture aux XIXe et XXe siècles. Paris, H. Laurens, Manuels d'histoire de l'art, 1928, in-8°.
NIEHAUS (Kasper). — Daumier en Millet, Amsterdam, 1928.
HOPPE (Ragnar). — Honoré Daumier, Gustave Courbet. « Forenfransk Konst » collection, Stockholm, 1929.
LARAN (Jean). — Cent vingt lithographies d'Honoré Daumier. Paris, Les Beaux-Arts, 1929, in-folio.
RIM (Carlo). — Honoré Daumier, son œuvre. Paris (*Nouvelle Revue Critique,* « Célébrités contemporaines », I, n° 5, 1929, in-8°).
CATALOGUE des estampes modernes, caricatures et scènes de mœurs. Lithographs by Daumier, Gavarni, Monnier. Gustave Cahen collection, Paris, 1929, in-4°.
ESCHOLIER (Raymond). — Daumier. Paris, Floury, « Anciens et Modernes », 1930, in-8°.
FUCHS (Eduard). — Der Maler Daumier (supplément). Munich, Albert Langen, 1930, small in-folio.
CATALOGUE of the Museum of Modern Art, New-York. Eighth Loan Exhibition : Corot and Daumier. Introduction by A. H. Barr Jr. New-York, 1930.
FOCILLON (Henri). — Les maîtres de l'estampe. Paris, H. Laurens, 1930, in-8°.
Daumier. Physionomies et physiologies. 81 wood-cuts after Daumier by E. Dété. Preface and catalogue of the wood-cuts of Daumier by Louis Dimier. Paris, Émile Nourry, 1930, in-4°.
BLANCHE (J.-E.). — La IIIe République. Vol. VIII : Les Arts Plastiques. Preface by Maurice Denis. Paris, *Les Editions de France,* 1931, in-8°.
GRASS-MICK (A.). — La lumière sur Daumier. Études sur l'artiste et son œuvre. Histoire de sa maison natale... Marseille, Tacussel, 1931, in-8°.
BOUVY (E.). — Trente-six bustes de Daumier. Paris, 1932.
CATALOGUE of the Exhibition of French art in the Royal Academy. London, 1932.
BOUVY (E.). — Daumier, l'œuvre gravé. Reproductions of all the plates. Notices and index. Paris, 1933, 2 volumes.
FOSCA (François). — Daumier. Paris, Plon, « Les maîtres de l'Art », 1933, in-8°.
CATALOGUE de l'Exposition Daumier au Musée de l'Orangerie, edited by Charles Sterling. Preface by Anatole de Monzie. Introduction by Claude Roger-Marx. Paris, 1934, in-16.
CATALOGUE de l'Exposition Daumier à la Bibliothèque Nationale. Notices by Julien Cain, P.-A. Lemoine and Jean Laran. Paris 1934.
FAURE (Élie). — Le *Don Quichotte* de Daumier in *Ombres Solides,* Paris, Malfère, 1934, in-16.
SCHEIWILLER (Giovanni). — Honoré Daumier. With a complete bibliographical essay. Milan, Hoepli, 1936.
CATALOGUE of the sale of the Oscar Schmitz Collection. Paris, Wildenstein, 1936.
CATALOGUE of the Daumier Exhibition. Pennsylvania Museum of Art. Preface by Claude Roger-Marx. Philadelphia, 1937.
MARX (Claude Roger-). — Daumier. Paris, Plon, « Les maîtres d'histoire et d'art », 1938.

ARTICLES

DURANTY. — Daumier (*La Gazette des Beaux-Arts*, May and June 1878) ; Daumier, son point de départ, sa vie, son talent (*Beaux-Arts illustrés*, 1879, n° 5).

MONTROSIER (Eugène). — La caricature politique. Honoré Daumier (*L'Art*, 1878, II, 25).

PELLETAN (Camille). — Exposition des œuvres de Daumier (*Le Rappel*, 1st February, 19, 23 and 29 April, 31 May 1878) ; Mort de Daumier (*Le Rappel*, 14 February 1879).

CARDON (Emile). — Profils d'artistes. Daumier (*Le Soleil illustré*, 14 April 1938).

FOUCHER (Paul). — Exposition de Daumier (*Le National*, 19 April, 1878) ; Mort de Daumier (*Le National*, 13 February 1879).

LEFORT (Paul). — Exposition de Daumier (*L'Evénement*, 19 and 23 April, 15 and 16 June 1878).

PUISSANT (G.). — Exposition de Daumier (*La Lanterne*, 20 April 1878).

VERON (Pierre). — Exposition de Daumier (*Charivari*, 20 April 1878) ; Mort de Daumier (*Charivari*, 13 February, 1879 ; *Journal Amusant*, 22 February, 1879).

BERTALL. — Exposition de Daumier (*Paris-Journal*, 21 April 1878)

SEBILLOT. — H. Daumier (*Le Bien public*, 23 April 1878).

VACHON (Marius). — H. Daumier (*La France*, 25 April 1878).

CASTAGNARY. — Exposition de Daumier (*Le Siècle*, 25 April 1878).

BERGERAT (Émile). — Exposition de Daumier (*Journal officiel*, 26 April 1878).

BURTY (Philippe). — Exposition de Daumier (*République Française*, 1st May 1878) ; Enterrement de Daumier (*République Française*, 15 February 1879).

LEROY (Louis). — Exposition Daumier (*Charivari*, 1st May 1878) ; Mort de Daumier (*Charivari*, 18 February 1879).

VIOLLET-LE-DUC. — L'œuvre de Daumier (*XIXᵉ Siècle*, 18 May 1878).

SURMAY (Paul).— Honoré Daumier (*Musée Universel*, 1st June 1878).

LAURENT (Charles). — Daumier (*La France*, 12 February 1879).

WOLFF (Albert). — Courrier de Paris. La mort de Daumier (*Le Figaro*, 13 February 1879).

VACQUERIE (A.). — Note nécrologique (*Le Rappel*, 13 February 1878).

FOUCHER (Paul). — Honoré Daumier (*Le National*, 13 February 1879).

BAZIRE (Edmond). — Les obsèques de Daumier. Discours de Champfleury et de Carjat (*Le Rappel*, 15 February 1879 ; *Beaux-Arts Illustrés*, 1879, n° 5).

BANVILLE (Th. de). — La Comédie moderne. Honoré Daumier. (*Le National*, 17 February 1879) ; Les Grands Chroniqueurs : Gavarni, Daumier, Cham (*Gil Blas*, 19 December 1879).

BLANC (Charles). — Duc, Daumier, Couture (*Le Temps*, 12 April 1879).

CLARETIE (Jules). — Courrier de la semaine (*L'Indépendance belge*, February 1879).

COQUIOT (Gustave). — Daumier (*Revue Universelle*, 1901, pp. 457-461).

GEFFROY (Gustave). — Daumier (*Revue de l'Art ancien et moderne*, 1901, IX, pp. 229-250) ; Daumier, sculpteur (*L'Art et les Artistes*, 1905, I, pp. 101-108).

ROSENTHAL (Léon). — Notes sur Daumier (*Bulletin de la Société de l'histoire de l'art français*, 1911, fasc. 4, pp. 351-352).

THACKERAY (W. M.). — Daumier's Robert Macaire (*The Print Collector's Quarterly*, London, 1914, vol. IV, n° 1).

BLUM (André). — La caricature sous la Monarchie de Juillet (*La Gazette des Beaux-Arts*, March-April 1920) ; Daumier ou la caricature politique en France sous la Seconde République (*L'Amateur d'Estampes*, 1923, n° 2 and 3).

MARX (Claude ROGER-). — Daumier au Louvre. Une rétrospective qui s'impose (*L'Humanité*, 14 December 1920) ; La leçon de Daumier au Salon d'Automne (*L'Information*, 7 November, 1921) ; Les croquis de Daumier (*Feuillets d'Art*, December 1921) ; Les lithographies de Daumier (*Le Journal*, 3 January 1922) ; Les dessins de Daumier (*Chanteclair*, September 1926) ; Le Cinquantenaire de la mort de Daumier (*L'Illustration*, 1929) ; Les dernières lithographies de Daumier (*L'Art vivant*, 1930, pp. 433-434); Daumier, illustrateur (*Arts et Métiers graphiques*, 15 September 1932, n° 31) ; H. Daumier (1934, 4 April 1934) ; The Daumier Exhibition. The Studio, London, 1934.

FONTAINAS (André). — Daumier (*L'Amour de l'Art*, October 1921).

SOFFICI (Ardengo). — Daumier pittore (*Dedalo*, Florence, November 1921).

DAYOT (Armand). — Honoré Daumier lithographe, peintre et sculpteur (*La Revue rhénane*, April-May 1923).

TATLOCK (R. R.). — Daumier (*The Burlington Magazine*, London, 1923, vol. 43, pp. 308-311).

SCHEFFLER (Karl). — Honoré Daumier. Exposition à la Galerie Matthiesen à Berlin (*L'Amour de l'Art*, May 1926).

DORMOY (Marie). — La collection Schmitz à Dresde (*L'Amour de l'Art*, October 1926) ; Un ensemble unique de cinquante Daumier. La collection Bureau (*Bulletin de l'Art ancien et moderne*, 1927, pp. 73-75).

FELS (Florent). — Images : Robert Macaire (*L'Art vivant*, 1st. August 1926).

FOSCA (François). — Les Daumier de la collection Bureau (*L'Amour de l'Art*, May 1927) ; La collection Claude Roger-Marx (*L'Amour de l'Art*, September 1929).

ZERVOS (Christian). — Idéalisme et naturalisme dans la peinture moderne. I. Corot, Courbet, Daumier (*Cahiers d'Art*, 1927, n° 9) ; Revisions : Daumier (*Cahiers d'Art*, 1930, n° 5).

TOZZI (Mario). — Cose Parigine : Corot, Renoir, Daumier (*Le Arti Plastiche*, Milan, 1st. January 1928).

ECKSTEIN (Hans). — Daumier. Die Kunst, Munich, 1928-1929, pp. 207-208. Corot Daumier Exhibition of the Museum of Modern Art, Parnassus, New-York, October 1930.

RAKUIT (W.). — Une exposition Daumier à Marseille (*L'Art et les Artistes*, 1928-1929, p. 110) ; On the Fiftieth Anniversary of Daumier's Death, Apollo, London, 1929, II, pp. 40-42.

FOCILLON (Henri). — Honoré Daumier, 1808-1879 (*La Gazette des Beaux-Arts*, 1929, II, pp. 79-104).

RIM (Carlo). — Le Cinquantenaire de Daumier (*L'Art vivant*, 15 February 1929).

BOUVY (E.). — Daumier et la *Revue des Deux Mondes* (*L'Amateur d'estampes*, 1931, pp. 59-62) ; Autour des bois de Daumier (*L'Amateur d'estampes*, 1931, pp. 74-82, 119-123, 153-156, 181-188, 1932, pp. 21-24, 40-50, 187-192) ; Daumier inconnu (*L'Amateur d'estampes*, 1934, p. 123).

MERYEM (Jean). — Quelques notes sur Daumier (*L'Art et les Artistes*, 1932, n° 131).

MARCHIORI (Giuseppe). — Omaggio a Daumier (*L'Orto*, Bologna, May 1933).

CLÉMENT-JANIN. — Daumier et ses graveurs (*Beaux-Arts*, 9 March 1934).

DIOLE (Philippe). — Daumier (*Beaux-Arts*, 16 March 1934).

NEUGASS (Fritz). — Honoré Daumier (*Die Weltkunst*, Berlin, 1st. April 1934).

ADHÉMAR (Jean). — Peut-on dater les peintures de Daumier ? (*Beaux-Arts*, 20 April 1934) ; Les légendes de Daumier (*L'Amateur d'estampes*, 1934, p. 54).

ZAHAR (Marcel). — Five loans made to the Exhibition of Daumier's work (*The Art News*, New-York, 21 April 1934).

VENTURI (Lionello). — Daumier (*L'Arte*, Turin, September 1934).

MONGAN (Agnès). — Six aquarelles inédites de Daumier (*La Gazette des Beaux-Arts*, 1st. September 1937, p. 245).

THE READER
Photo Hyperion

HEAD OF A BELL-RINGER
Photo Studios Limited

CHILD WITH A DOLL
Photo Vizzavona

PORTRAIT OF A PAINTER
Photo Vizzavona

THE SINGING COUPLE
Photo Bulloz

PORTRAIT OF A WOMAN
Photo Vizzavona

HEAD OF SCAPIN
Photo Vizzavona

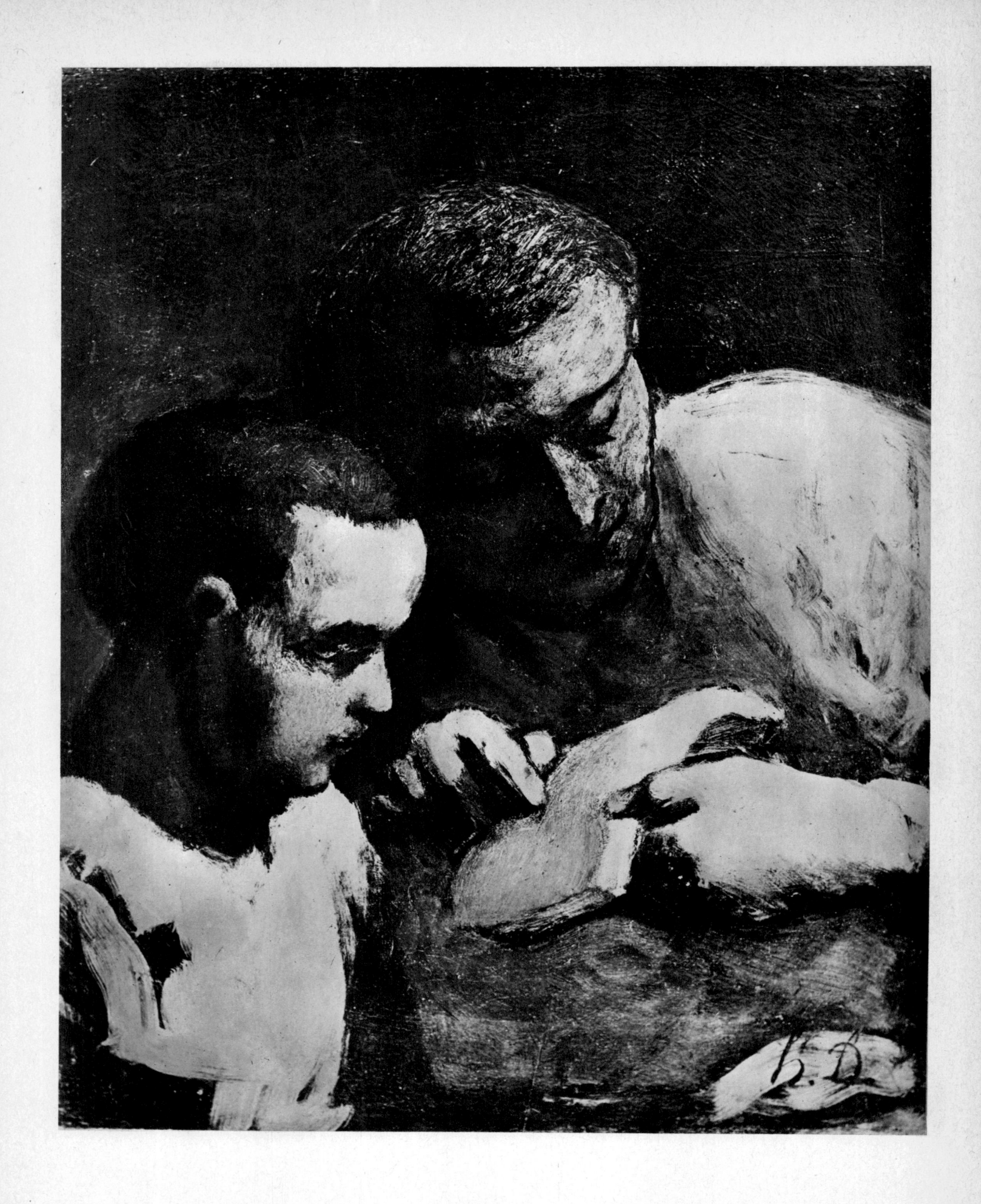

READING
Photo Durand-Ruel

THE CHESS-PLAYERS
Photo Hyperion

THE BEER-DRINKERS
Photo Bulloz

THE SMOKER
Photo Vizzavona

IN THE WINE-SHOP
Photo Bernheim Jeune

THE TOPERS
Photo Durand-Ruel

AT THE CAFÉ
Photo Rosenberg

THE TOPERS
Photo Druet

THE SCULPTOR'S STUDIO
Photo Durand-Ruel

48

THE PAINTER
Photo Hyperion

CAMILLE COROT
Photo Durand-Ruel

POLITICS
Photo Durand-Ruel

THE THREE AMATEURS
Photo Giraudon

THE SERENADE
Photo A. C. Cooper

THE ARTIST BEFORE HIS WORK
Photo Bulloz

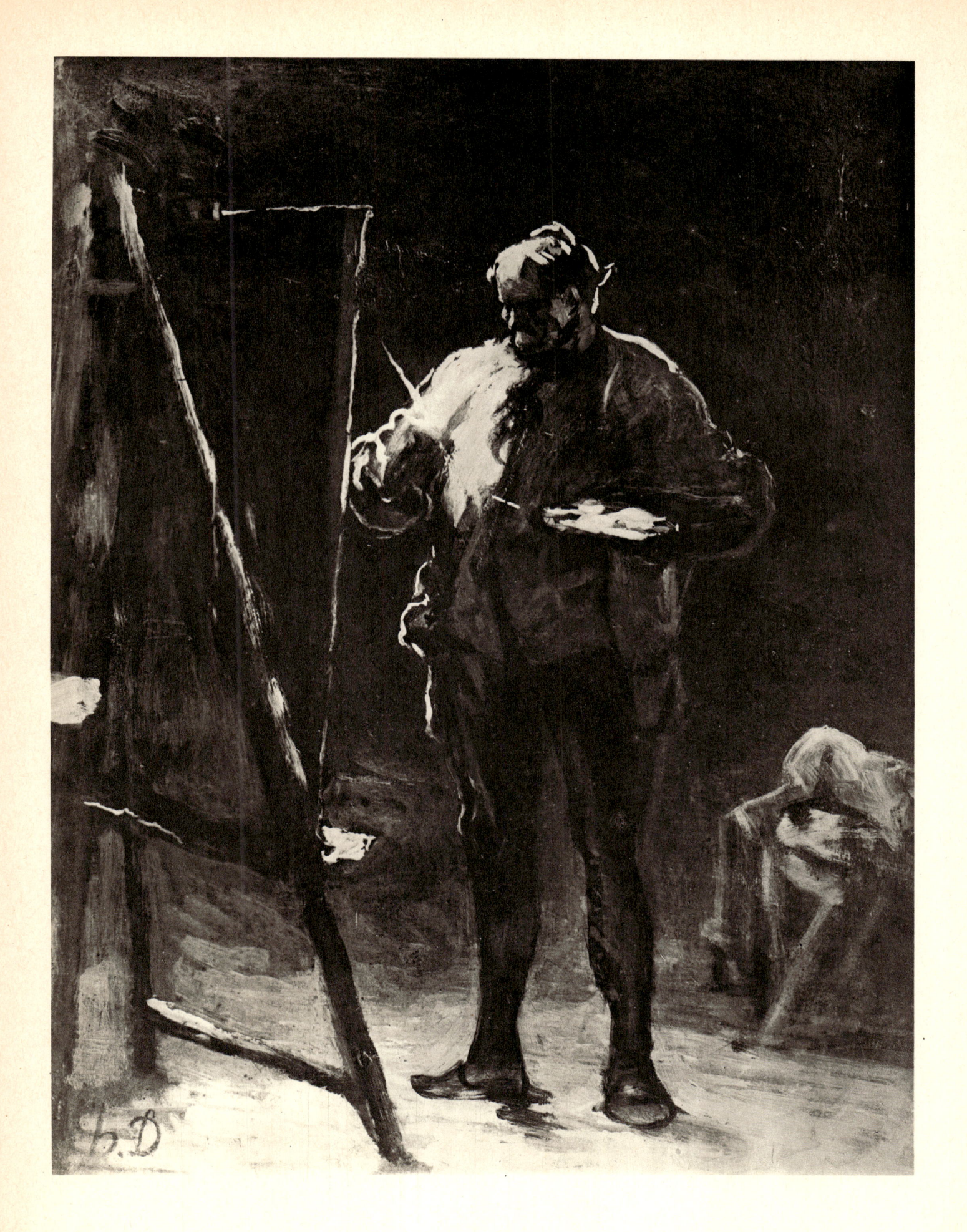

THE PAINTER
Photo Vizzavona

55

THE PRINT COLLECTOR
Photo Giraudon

THE PRINT COLLECTOR
Photo Hyperion

PRINT COLLECTORS
Photo Gold

58

THE CONNOISSEURS
Photo Rosenberg

THE PRINT COLLECTOR
Photo Druet

THE PRINT COLLECTOR
Photo Druet

61

THE CURIOUS
Photo Druet

BEFORE THE PRINT-SELLER'S
Photo Durand-Ruel

63

BEFORE THE PRINT-SELLER'S
Photo Giraudon

BEFORE THE PRINT-SELLER'S
Photo Hyperion

65

IN A PAINTER'S STUDIO
Photo Durand-Ruel

THE COLLECTOR
Photo Durand-Ruel

THREE COLLECTORS EXAMINING A LITHOGRAPH BY RAFFET
Photo Bulloz

THE PRINT COLLECTORS
Photo Bulloz

THE LISTENER
Photo Vizzavona

HUNTERS BEFORE THE FIRE
Photo Bulloz

71

A VISIT TO THE STUDIO
Photo Druet

PRINT COLLECTORS
Photo Hyperion

THREE LAWYERS TALKING
Photo Druet

THE TWO LAWYERS
Photo Vizzavona

CONVERSATION BETWEEN LAWYERS
Photo Bulloz

"MY DEAR FELLOW!"
Photo Durand-Ruel

THE SPEECH
Photo Vizzavona

AFTER THE HEARING
Photo Durand-Ruel

79

THE CONSEQUENTIAL LAWYER
Photo Bernheim

A LAWYER READING
Photo Hyperion

LAWYER AND CLIENT
Photo Bernheim Jeune

TWO LAWYERS TALKING
Photo Vizzavona

AFTER THE VERDICT
Photo Giraudon

THE LAWYERS
Photo Bernheim Jeune

THE ARTICLES PRODUCED IN EVIDENCE
Photo Durand-Ruel

86

FORGIVENESS
Photo Giraudon

87

A FAMILY ON THE BARRICADE
Photo Druet

COMING OUT OF SCHOOL
Photo Hyperion

SOUP
Photo Druet

THE SECRET
Photo Vizzavona

91

THE BOAT-TOWER
Photo Vizzavona

92

THE BEGGARS
Photo Bernheim Jeune

THE WASHERWOMEN
Photo Heinrich Klette

THE MARKET
Photo Bulloz

THE BURDEN
Photo Giraudon

THE WASHERWOMAN
Photo Hyperion

THE WATER-CARRIER
Photo Druet

THE HOUSE-PAINTER
Photo Bulloz

THE BUTCHER
Photo Bulloz

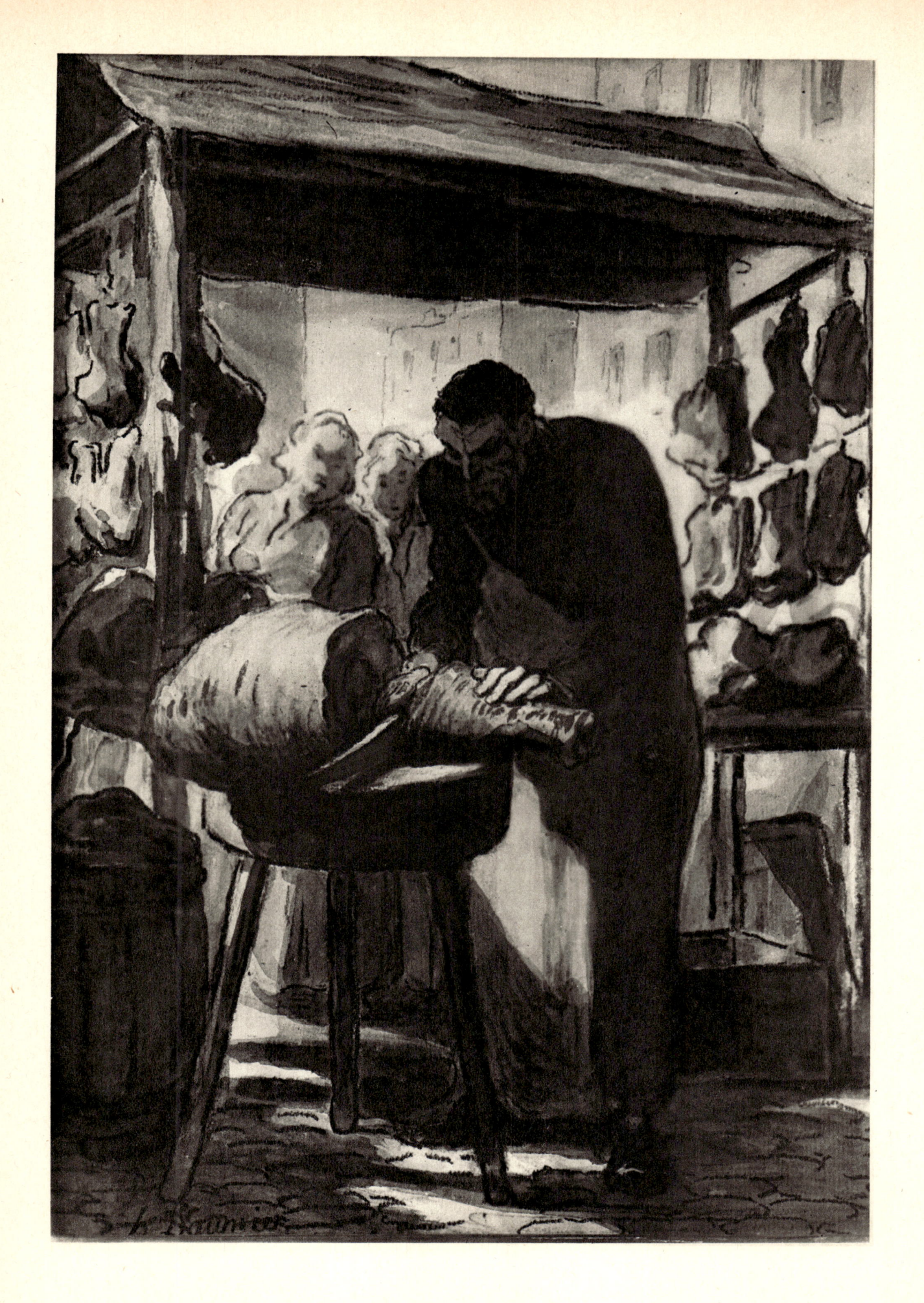

THE PORK-BUTCHER
Photo Druet

101

SAVED!
Photo Vizzavona

BATHER
Photo Gauthier

CHILDREN PLAYING
Photo Wildenstein

YOUNG GIRL AND CHILD
Photo Hyperion

BATHING
Photo Druet

106

AFTER THE BATHE
Photo Wildenstein

NUDE CHILDREN
Photo Druet

THE BATHERS
Photo Vizzavona

PASSERS-BY
Photo Giraudon

COMPOSITION
Photo Bernheim Jeune

111

THE EMIGRANTS
Photo Vizzavona

THE EMIGRANTS
Photo Hyperion

THE WATERING-PLACE
Photo Gold

HORSEMEN
Photo Druet

115

HORSEMEN IN THE FOREST
Photo Druet

SUNDAY MORNING
Photo Gold

117

THE KISS
Photo Giraudon

OEDIPUS AND THE SHEPHERD
Photo Bulloz

THE THIEVES AND THE ASS
Photo Giraudon

MARY MAGDALEN
Photo Hyperion

THE SECOND CLASS CARRIAGE
Photo Foto-Press

THE THIRD CLASS CARRIAGE
Photo Durand-Ruel

123

THE THIRD CLASS CARRIAGE
Photo Druet

THE THIRD CLASS CARRIAGE
Photo Bernheim Jeune

125

THE WAITING-ROOM
Photo Paul Rosenberg

THE NIGHT-WANDERERS
Photo Vizzavona

127

ORCHESTRA STALLS
Photo Vizzavona

THE AUDIENCE
Photo Hyperion

COMING OUT OF THE THEATRE
Photo Druet

THE AUDIENCE
Photo Vizzavona

THE INTERVAL
Photo Druet

AT THE THEATRE
Photo Durand-Ruel

AT THE THEATRE
Photo Vizzavona

AT THE THEATRE
Photo Wildenstein

PIERROT PLAYING THE GUITAR
Photo Gold

SCENE FROM A PLAY
Photo Hyperion

THE DRAMA
Photo Druet

A FREE SHOW
Photo Durand-Ruel

THEATRE SCENE
Photo Wildenstein

140

"LE MALADE IMAGINAIRE"
Photo Durand-Ruel

141

SCENE FROM A PLAY
Photo Bernheim Jeune

CRISPIN AND SCAPIN
Photo Druet

HEAD OF PASQUIN
Photo Durand-Ruel

144

CLOWN
Photo Hyperion

THE MOUNTEBANKS AT REST
Photo Druet

146

THE MOUNTEBANKS PARADE
Photo Bulloz

147

THE SHOW
Photo Durand-Ruel

148

THE SHOW
Photo Bulloz

MOUNTEBANKS MOVING
Photo Bulloz

THE STREET-SINGERS
Photo Giraudon

THE STRONG MAN OF THE FAIR
Photo Foto-Press

THE SHOW
Photo Hyperion

DON QUIXOTE
Photo Druet

DON QUIXOTE AND SANCHO PANZA
Photo Druet

DON QUIXOTE PRANCING BEFORE SANCHO PANZA
Photo Bulloz

DON QUIXOTE IN THE MOUNTAINS
Photo Druet

DON QUIXOTE AND SANCHO PANZA
Photo Bernheim Jeune

DON QUIXOTE AND SANCHO PANZA
Photo Vizzavona

DON QUIXOTE READING
Photo Bernheim

DAUMIER AND THE CRITICS

It is often best for a great artist to come into conflict during his life-time with savage prejudices, and to be the victim of intrigues and hostile campaigns. For when these obstacles are overcome, the truth is revealed, and his fame shines out. By contrast, it is perhaps possible to explain the public's obstinate disregard of Daumier's work as a painter by the fact that the artist never aroused such feelings while at the same time he won the good opinion of his best contemporaries; and also by the fact that for another section of his work, he had experienced a crushing celebrity. It is obviously more difficult to enlighten opinion and direct it when it is already formed, than to set right a crying wrong.

On the other hand, Daumier seldom revealed himself as a painter, and it needed Baudelaire, in his writings on Daumier's engraved work, to foresee, with the insight of genius, the pictorial faculties which he was later to show. Nevertheless, Daumier did compete, in 1848, for an officially-commissioned picture representing the Republic.

At the Salon, he exhibited in 1849 « The Robbers and the Donkey » (*Les voleurs et l'Ane*); in 1850 and 1851 « Women pursued by a Satyr » (*Des femmes poursuivies par un satyre*) and « Don Quixote and Sancho going to the wedding of Cramacho » (*Don Quichotte et Sancho se rendant aux noces de Cramache*); and in 1861, « A Washerwoman » (*Une blanchisseuse*). These works attracted little attention. Comments were confined to mentioning the difficulties Daumier was struggling against in painting—it is a case of Baudelaire saying to Delacroix that Daumier was unable to achieve any finish, of Champfleury talking of « the restlessness of brushwork that tires itself out in useless repetitions and re-touchings. » However, a drawing of « The Drunkenness of Silenus » (*L'Ivresse de Silène*) (1860) is described by the Goncourts in their journal.

« Behind the God, who is being carried or rather dragged along, are floating draperies, arms waved in the air hailing with echoing cries those fellow-revellers, who, in the distance behind the forest, are breaking into a countryside loud with the news of fresh-made wine. What ebullience, what profusion in this satiric drama among a myriad leaves! What untiring improvisation! What broad, frank shouts of laughter, laughter that reveals everywhere flashing teeth, laughter that always rings true, like the laughter of the good old times, the Golden Age. There is an expansion of energy there, a healthy jollity, a natural go, a four-square character, a puissant animality and something of the freedom and toughness of Old France which perhaps one might look for in vain elsewhere than in Rabelais. »

Again, on the 13th of April 1865, the Goncourts note that they have « seen going down the Rue Laffitte some terrific Daumier watercolours. The water-colours represent Panathenaic congresses of the legal faculty, meetings between barristers, processions of judges; the backgrounds are lurid, lit with the grim daylight of police-magistrates' offices, or the greyness of some corridor in the law-courts. They are in washes of indian ink applied with feverish fantasy. The heads are hideous, with an exultation, a joviality, that is frightening. There is an indescribable horror about these black-gowned figures, as of antique masks grinning in a registry-office. The smiles of solicitors take on a corybantic air, the most sinister of the barristers have about them something that is faun-like. »

In 1869, Daumier again exhibited three water-colours of lawyers, doctors and magistrates. « In connection with these, » Duranty reports, « M. Bonvin, (the painter, represented in the Duveen Room at the Tate Gallery) appealed to the selection committee through the medium of the press to grant some award to a man who he said was of the same importance as Goya and Hogarth, if not more. »

For many years the public had no further chance of seeing Daumier's painting; it was known only to a few friends and initiates. It was not till 1878 that Daumier's friends organised the famous exhibition at Durand Ruel's gallery, where there were ninety-four of his paintings, a hundred and thirty-nine of his water-colours and drawings, most of his sculpture and the greater part of his lithographs, which were shown in relays and changed from week to week. This exhibition, while not visited by an influx of the public, gave the critics an opportunity to show their interest. They responded with an intelligence and understanding which deserve to be underlined. Even discounting the political sympathies which weighed in Daumier's favour, one may quote from most of the articles published on that occasion critical opinions of considerable value. For instance Camille Pelletan wrote in *Le Rappel* a whole series of articles, in one of which (May 31st 1878) he compares the art of Daumier with the whole of the exhibited examples of European Painting at the Universal Exhibition. He says « I find in these paintings, all of very broad execution, most of them left as mere sketches, something I can find nowhere else; the forceful interpretation of modern life. Quay-side scenes, with washerwomen, women drawing water, and incidents of all sorts taken from the world about us are treated with the same grandeur and the same truth. The style has some affinity with that of Delacroix, some with that of Millet, but it nevertheless remains individual... the artist has given us a broad transcription of contemporary manners; he has elicited the underlying reality of what he sees; his style has a greatness which is almost classic, but with an entirely modern flavour. » On Daumier's work as a draughtsman, he writes elsewhere (April 29th 1879).

« At the Exhibition, the authorities have had the idea of placing side by side with the finished work some of those rapid sketches which exhibit the artist's thought in the very process of creation. Daumier is here at his most masterly, in the full pride of his first intentions, by virtue of the accuracy and breadth of his indications, and by the gift he has of bringing out in his figures the noblest attitudes in a few strokes done with incredible brilliance. Amid the floating network of strokes in which the idea is being felt for, one perceives the master-contours in all their power and truth... In place of a dry and minutely-drawn outline, one can see, among these suggestions boldly indicated with strong touches of the chalk, the broad masses standing out in strong relief. One can well understand that an artist with such a sense of modelling should have wanted to solidify his conceptions in the plasticity of clay... let us take the fine series of heads and shoulders in terra-cotta from Mme Philippon's collection. Leonardo da Vinci made, in his note-books, caricatures in which this or that structural deformity of feature, thought of partly of course from a scientific point of view, gives an extraordinary effect of the comic. Many of Daumier's subjects give an analogous impression. »

Most of the press criticisms repeat similar opinions. Duranty took advantage of the occasion to publish in the *Gazette des Beaux-Arts* a full and illustrated study of all Daumier's work. The second edition (June 1878) is specially devoted to the artist's drawings and paintings. « His dream was painting, and it is only since 1864, or thereabouts, that he has been able to fondle it and nurse it into realisation at his leisure... With the exception of a few canvases, it might be said that the whole of his work as a painter is in essence drawing in paint or colours. Often the outlines of his designs are emphasized with strong black lines; the strokes of pen or charcoal mingle with wash or water-colour. The colourist seems to have grown out of the draughtsman. It is with the black and white of the chalk-drawing that he has made himself so intimately conversant with the brilliance of light and the depths of shadow. Though he may in a secondary degree concern himself with the beauty of particular tones, the foundation of his colouring proceeds none the less essentially from the larger masses and half-tones which black-and-white has the advantage of summing up and emphasizing. The lighting in his paintings has therefore almost always a suggestion of moonlight, and consists of shades of clarety lilac and greenish or bluish grey, not far removed in tone from the white of paper. Thus, whether in his black and whites, his paintings or his coloured drawings Daumier works in broad effects in which detail is lost, in which figures and movements are set down and developed with rapidity in a general and powerful flow of impetus, or are sometimes quietened down beneath a veil of tender shadow. As he worked in lithography, so he drew and painted... there is a great display of charcoal or wash, and great areas of single tones, russet, buff, blue-grey, blue-black, or white, balancing each other. The paintings, drawings and lithographs make a united and indivisible whole. In painting, he made many researches and some tentative experiments; but throughout all the attempts he made he was guided and sustained by his fine feeling for modelling in monumental planes. »

So one sees that there was already a real consensus of opinion about Daumier's work. This exhibition of 1878 had all the atmosphere of a retrospective one-man show. As a matter of fact the artist who had then for sometime been blind was soon to die. There was a renewal of critical enthusiasm. In a leading article in the « Figaro » (13 th Feb. 1879) Albert Wolff, who was later to make himself so ridiculous by his opinions on Impressionism, devotes a long article to Daumier, full of feeling and insight.

« Public opinion refused with the obstinacy of ignorance to recognise the undeniable power of this astonishing draughtsman and the unusual energy of his painting. Where the man in the street saw nothing but a comic strip, painters unreservedly acclaimed a power of drawing reminiscent, in more than one instance, of the great masters. This mere caricaturist showed a grasp of the human form in the nude superior to that of the gentlemen of the Beaux-Arts academy who claimed the monopoly of such knowledge. No one knew better than Daumier how to construct a human body and give it relief in a few strokes of the pencil... A great man misunderstood, he nevertheless knew his own value perfectly well.

His outward timidity and resignation concealed a great sense of pride; the best men of his time recognised his talent... he had as friends and devoted admirers three men of whom French Art had reason to be proud — Jules Dupré, Corot and Daubigny. »

In the « Temps » of the 12th of April 1879, an equally important article coupled the names of Daumier and Couture. No doubt its object was to deplore the fact that the caricaturist's popularity was greater than that of the painter (although Couture had been loaded with far more official honours than Daumier). But these notes, though intentionally bitter and pointed, finally redound to the greater glory of Daumier. Charles Blanc deprecates his repetitions, his caricatures of the antique, and his so-called attempts at the grand manner. But he also writes:

« There is a touch both of Rembrandt and of Goya in Daumier. His lithographs are always enlivened by a colourful chiaroscuro. His touch with the chalk is rich and oily, and crumbles on the stone with mordant accents of black that are mysterious and sometimes of tragic power. If he opens his window on to the surrounding countryside, he can sketch with facility and feeling a landscape which he well knows how to invest with picturesqueness, atmosphere and space. A remarkable thing about his caricatures is that they are made without models, without the assistance of nature which he is nevertheless able to remember as though it were present. His technique is of the sort that is carried along by imagination instead of being tied down to the actual. Delacroix was very fond, among Daumier's works, of the « Bathers » series, and often had occasion to copy them. »

In 1888 there appeared the first monograph devoted to Daumier. It is signed Arsène Alexandre, and still remains to-day the basis of all studies of the artist. His entire work is examined in it, in detail, and a quantity of information is transmitted to us about the man and his methods of work. Arsène Alexandre puts Daumier in exactly his right place when he writes:

« It is this original side of his work (i. e. painting) which finally makes him the equal of the most famous, and will open the portals of all the Museums for him when the impartial judgement of posterity has rid the nineteenth century of many other exaggerated reputations... He might have been a sort of Teniers with Delacroix's vigour... He is as rich as a colourist as he is penetrating as an observer and skilful as a draughtsman. A colourist indeed, but with the slightest possible means... his palette is as economical as possible. Brown, black, white and red suffice him almost exclusively in obtaining the warmest and most varied effects... he chooses a tone as simple and yet at the same time as deep as possible, and then by the mere use of gradations, passing invariably from the lightest to the strongest, he extracts from this dominant tone all that it is possible to get from it. In a word he has the surest and most ingenious possible sense of values. »

But none the less, in spite of these articles and the abovementioned monograph, in spite of this clear consensus of opinions, and in spite of the growing value it has in the eyes of collectors, Daumier's painting is still unrecognised by the taste of the public. The old caricaturist legend about Daumier tenaciously survives. Apparently the battle will never be definitely won. On the occasion of the Universal Exhibition of 1900, the splendid exhibition of a hundred years of French Art gave an important place to Daumier (nineteen works). It was a fresh surprise, as though the 1878 Exhibition had never taken place. It was possible for Roger Marx to write.

« There is a sovereign irony in his watercolours of doctors, collectors, and lawyers; the sad thing is that they should have absorbed all the attention and admiration. Except for an elect few, no one took any notice of his pictures, and now we see that they are of primary importance, worthy in their moral implications, of a Molière or a Balzac. The Centenary exhibition of 1900 would have been worth while if only for having proclaimed the equality of Daumier with the masters of the art of painting. »

The lessons of the 1900 Exhibition do not appear however to have had the widespread influence that might have been expected. Although Daumier's reputation continually grew abroad, especially in Germany, and although a number of learned works were published and catalogues of lithographs and paintings drawn up, it was still possible to read, though not without surprise, the following lines from the pen of a French critic of the importance of M. Louis Dimier:

« For the past twenty years these productions of his (the reference is to Daumier's work in oils) have been persistently belauded. This perversion of a talent justly celebrated for work of another kind has found much favour. It is the fashion nowadays to praise artists for things that lie outside their special province—as for instance the statuettes of Corot, the watercolours of a sculptor like Barye, the oil-paintings of Carpeaux another sculptor), and so on. As we have put Ingres' violins in the Pantheon, it is hardly surprising that it is now Daumier's turn, and that an artist whose whole career lay in lithography and wood-engraving, and whose attempts at painting were never seriously considered by his contemporaries, should have been promoted at a bound to the rank of master in respect of them. Thus canvasses, which neither Corot nor Delacroix nor Daubigny nor anyone else thought anything of, have been thrust on our notice; canvasses which in spite of the unheard-of fuss collectors have made about them, one discovers with extreme disappointment to be as uninteresting as ever... anyone with their eyes open could see that with few exceptions the master produced nothing of any value after 1848. »

It would be impossible that anyone, while proclaiming that the truth stared him in the face, should have his eyes more firmly shut than this. But no doubt M. Focillon is right when he explains the resistance to Daumier thus:—

« Had his name worn out its glory?—Possibly a stage of oblivion is necessary to true greatness. True, several painters of the proudest fame had particularly admired him. But even though traces of his example survive in the character of their achievement, Daumier soars beyond such horizons. He is a man in whose mind and art two virtues are enshrined in which we are cruelly lacking; the sense of mystery and the instinct of that heroism which is not without its tender, human side. It is this which will long render him proof against cockney wit, that flotsam which lives and dies on the surface of the deep waters of Parisian life. It is this by virtue of which his art, a thing unique in our history, continues the tradition of Rabelais through Balzac to join the dynasty of the masters of our country's spirit. »

The following lengthy study by M. Focillon which appeared in the *Gazette des Beaux-Arts* in 1929 abounds in interesting notes on the artist's technique:

« It is remarkable to observe how light, with Daumier, acts not only as an all-pervading medium but as an active and creative force. It governs the composition, and at the same time bestows life, breadth and energy on things and people. We are made to feel that the picture-space is not real space, but a medium of greater intensity and radiance in which appearances take on a new quality, as though they were moulded into a single whole by light and shade. In this golden glow we again see the advantages of his labours in black and white. The connexion between Daumier's painting and his lithographs and sculptures is of the same order as that which links up Rembrandt's paintings with his etchings. But Daumier is simpler and more sober. There is no halo round the source of the light in whose direct beams he bathes the creatures of his fancy... The daylight of the streets which illumines with such tragic rays the troubled sleep of his mountebanks, is enough for him; enough for him the stormy twilight which gilds, behind the washerwoman, the high tenements of our quay-sides; enough for him is the half-light which in the print-shop wakes into life before the collector's eyes the warmth of the red-chalk drawings which hang on the walls. His touch takes this light and shade and incorporates them in loveliest paint that ever was rich, solid, without useless aggressiveness, taking shape at a touch... Painting with him is a constructive element and no mere pleasantness of surface. Values, form and tone come to life with the same impetus and the same stroke of the brush, as though beneath the hand of a sculptor. » Thus a better understanding and a more just appreciation of Daumier's work is in spite of everything being worked out. The slow but sure reconquest of his fame is marked out in its various stages by numerous works. In Germany, the introductions to the catalogues of Klossowski and Fuchs; in France, the works of Henry Marcel, André Fontainas, Raymond Escholier and above all the absolutely conclusive work of François Fosca (1933). This work teems with original interpretations and just analogies between Daumier's work and the times in which he lived; literature, philosophy and morals are all touched upon. In fact, it is a particularly interesting attempt to assess the artist's place in history. According to François Fosca, Daumier would take his place in the current of French Baroque represented in painting by Lebrun and Jouvenet, in sculpture by Puget, in literature by Lamennais, Hugo and Michelet.

It would be a terrestrial baroque as in Ribera or Rubens, as opposed to the celestial baroque of Tintoretto, Greco, and Bernini; Rembrandt « remaining as always, in isolation, and connecting up with both groups. »

We may also mention the activities of Claude Roger-Marx, one of the best connoisseurs of Daumier, who for years has shown himself a positively militant champion in the artist's cause, through articles, the organisation of exhibitions, and lastly the recent work he has published, which is extremely precise and well-documented. But it is undoubtedly the most effective attitude to let Daumier and his work speak for themselves. The exhibition at the Musée de l'Orangerie in 1934 has probably done more for the knowledge and understanding of Daumier than many monographs, even the best. It must now be left to a French Museum to make permanent and lasting the work which, in its humble way, this album of reproductions of Daumier's work in painting has attempted in some measure to adumbrate.

DETAILED DESCRIPTION OF THE PLATES AND REPRODUCTIONS

33. THE READER. Wood, 34 by 26 cm. Paul Rosenberg collection, Paris. Photo Hyperion.
34. HEAD OF A BELL-RINGER. 35 by 27 cm. Formerly A. Alexandre collection. Private collection, England. Photo Studios Limited.
35. CHILD WITH A DOLL. Private collection. Photo Vizzavona.
36. PORTRAIT OF A PAINTER. Canvas, 29 by 18,5 cm. Private collection, Paris. Photo Vizzavona.
37. THE SINGING COUPLE. Wood, 56 by 46 cm. Rijksmuseum, Amsterdam. Photo Bulloz.
38. PORTRAIT OF A WOMAN. 40 by 32 cm. Formerly O. Mirbeau collection. The Dumbarton Oaks collection, United States. Photo Vizzavona.
39. HEAD OF SCAPIN. Wood, 33 by 26 cm. Formerly A. Alexandre collection. Private collection, Paris. Photo Vizzavona.
40. READING. 27 by 22 cm. Private collection. Photo Durand-Ruel.
41. THE CHESS-PLAYERS. Wood, 24 by 33 cm. Formerly Jacquette collection. Palais des Beaux-Arts de la Ville de Paris. Photo Hyperion.
42. THE BEER-DRINKERS. Wood, 22,5 by 27 cm. Mme Esnault-Pelterie's collection. Photo Bulloz.
    TWO HEADS. Drawing. Private collection.
43. THE SMOKER. Canvas, 26 by 33,5 cm. Formerly Georges Viau collection, Paris. Formerly Murray collection, Aberdeen. Photo Vizzavona.
    MAN SEATED. Drawing. Private collection.
44. IN THE WINE-SHOP. Water-colour, 22 by 30 cm. Formerly Somers and Coleman collections. Photo Bernheim Jeune.
    THE LAUGHER. Drawing. Private collection.
45. THE TOPERS. Water-colour, 25 by 35 cm. Private collection. Photo Durand-Ruel.
    HEAD. Drawing. Private collection.
46. AT THE CAFÉ. Wood, 27 by 35 cm. Formerly Hazard collection. O. Reinhardt collection, Winterthur. Photo Rosenberg.
    WORKMEN IN THE STREET. Wood, 12 by 16 cm. Formerly H. Rouart collection.
47. THE TOPERS. 37 by 28 cm. Formerly H. Rouart collection. Adolf Lewisohn collection, New-York. Photo Druet.
48. THE SCULPTOR'S STUDIO. Wood, 26 by 35 cm. Formerly Uhle collection, Dresden. Philips Memorial Gallery, Washington. Photo Durand-Ruel.
    DRAWING FROM A PLASTER MODEL. Claude Roger-Marx collection, Paris.
49. THE PAINTER. Wood, 26 by 34 cm. Musée de Reims. Photo Hyperion.
50. CAMILLE COROT. Water-colour, 32 by 24 cm. Metropolitan Museum, New-York. Photo Durand-Ruel.
51. POLITICS. Water-colour, 37 by 28 cm. Gerstenberg collection. Photo Durand-Ruel.
52. THE THREE AMATEURS. Wood, 22 by 25 cm. Formerly Jacquette collection. Palais de Beaux-Arts de la Ville de Paris. Photo Giraudon.
    HEAD. Drawing accentuated with wash. Claude Roger-Marx collection, Paris.
53. THE SERENADE. Collection of Sir Michael Sadleir. Photo A. C. Cooper.
    HEAD. Water-colour. Claude Roger-Marx collection, Paris.
54. THE ARTIST BEFORE HIS WORK. Water-colour, 38 by 29 cm. Formerly Jules Dupré collection. Photo Bulloz.
55. THE PAINTER. Wood, 33,5 by 26 cm. Private collection, Germany. Photo Vizzavona.
56. THE PRINT COLLECTOR. Canvas, 40 by 32 cm. Formerly Jacquette collection. Palais des Beaux-Arts de la Ville de Paris. Photo Giraudon.
57. THE PRINT COLLECTOR. Canvas, 16,5 by 21,5 cm. Longa collection, Paris. Photo Hyperion.
58. PRINT COLLECTORS. Wood, 21 by 16 cm. Formerly A. Alexandre collection. Photo Gold.
59. THE CONNOISSEURS. Canvas, 40 by 32 cm. Formerly Feydeau collection. Mrs. E. Jonas's collection, New-York. Photo Rosenberg.
60. THE PRINT COLLECTOR. Canvas, 40 by 31 cm. Formerly Corot and H. Rouart collections. Musée de Lyon. Photo Druet.
61. THE PRINT COLLECTOR. Wood, 40 by 32 cm. Formerly Georges Viau collection. Mme Doucet's collection, Paris. Photo Druet.
62. THE CURIOUS. Private collection. Photo Druet.
63. BEFORE THE PRINT-SELLER'S. Wood, 34 by 24 cm. Formerly Corot collection. Private collection, United States.
64. BEFORE THE PRINT-SELLER'S. 32 by 24 cm. Private collection. Photo Giraudon.
65. BEFORE THE PRINT-SELLER'S. Canvas, 33 by 24 cm. Formerly Lemaire collection. Mme Emile Staub-Terlinden's collection, Männedorf. Photo Hyperion.
66. IN A PAINTER'S STUDIO. Water-colour, 32,4 by 31 cm. Walters Art Gallery, Baltimore. Photo Durand-Ruel.
67. THE COLLECTOR. Water-colour, 44 by 35 cm. Formerly J. Dupré collection. Metropolitan Museum, New-York. Photo Durand-Ruel.
68. THREE COLLECTORS EXAMINING A LITHOGRAPH BY RAFFET. Water-colour, 26 by 31 cm. Musée du Louvre, Paris. Photo Bulloz.
    MAN SEATED IN AN ARM-CHAIR. Quill drawing, 21 by 18 cm. Claude Roger-Marx collection, Paris.
69. THE PRINT COLLECTORS. Private collection. Photo Bulloz.
    THE COLLECTOR. Private collection.
70. THE LISTENER. Quill and charcoal drawing accentuated with wash, 29 by 23 cm. Formerly H. Rouart collection. Gerstenberg collection. Photo Vizzavona.
71. HUNTERS BEFORE THE FIRE. Water-colour, 25 by 35 cm. Mme Esnault-Pelterie's collection. Photo Bulloz.
    HEAD. Quill drawing. Claude Roger-Marx collection, Paris.
72. A VISIT TO THE STUDIO. 39 by 31 cm. Formerly Corot and Tavernier collections. Photo Druet.
73. PRINT COLLECTORS. Canvas, 35 by 26 cm. Private collection, Switzerland. Photo Hyperion.
74. THREE LAWYERS TALKING. Canvas, 40 by 33 cm. Formerly H. Rouart collection. Philips Memorial Gallery, Washington. Photo Druet.
75. THE TWO LAWYERS. Canvas, 33 by 24 cm. Formerly H. Rouart collection. Musée de Lyon. Photo Vizzavona.
76. CONVERSATION BETWEEN LAWYERS. Water-colour, 26 by 21 cm. Formerly Bureau collection. Photo Bulloz.
77. « MY DEAR FELLOW! » Water-colour, 28 by 21 cm. National Gallery of Victoria, Melbourne. Photo Durand-Ruel.
78. THE SPEECH. Water-colour, 26,5 by 33 cm. Gerstenberg collection. Photo Vizzavona.
    DEBATE. Drawing in Indian ink. Private collection.
79. AFTER THE HEARING. Water-colour, 28 by 35 cm. Mme Esnault-Pelterie's collection. Photo Durand-Ruel.
    AN ENCOUNTER. Drawing in Indian ink. Private collection.
80. THE CONSEQUENTIAL LAWYER. Water-colour, 28 by 21 cm. Private collection. Photo Bernheim Jeune.
81. A LAWYER READING. Canvas, 39 by 31 cm. Formerly Corot and Tavernier collections. Dr. Robert Bühler's collection, Winterthür. Photo Hyperion.
82. LAWYER AND CLIENT. Water-colour, 16,5 by 22 cm. Formerly Castagnary collection. Photo Berhneim Jeune.

LAWYER AND CLIENT. Water-colour, 22 by 18 cm. Formerly Royer collection.
83. TWO LAWYERS TALKING. Wood, 21 by 27,5 cm. Private collection. Photo Vizzavona.
A LAWYER AND HIS CLIENT. Wood, 14 by 13 cm. Formerly Coleman collection.
84. AFTER THE VERDICT. Water-colour, 14 by 23 cm. Formerly Jacquette collection. Palais des Beaux-Arts de la Ville de Paris.
SKETCHES FOR COURT SCENES. Quill drawing. Claude Roger-Marx collection.
85. THE LAWYERS. Water-colour, 23 by 31 cm. J. N. Brown collection, Providence, L. I., U. S. A. Photo Bernheim Jeune.
A JUDGE. Water-colour, 15 by 10 cm. Max Silberberg collection.
86. THE ARTICLES PRODUCED IN EVIDENCE. Water-colour, 31,5 by 47 cm. National Gallery of Victoria, Melbourne. Photo Durand-Ruel.
THE JUDGES. Quill drawing, 10 by 12 cm.
87. FORGIVENESS. Wood, 36 by 68 cm. Formerly Bureau collection. J. Goldschmidt collection. Photo Giraudon.
A BROAD GESTURE. Quill drawing accentuated with wash. Private collection.
88. A FAMILY ON THE BARRICADE. Canvas, 84 by 73 cm. Formerly Georges Viau collection. Private collection, Copenhagen. Photo Druet.
89. COMING OUT OF SCHOOL. Wood, 40 by 31 cm. Formerly A. Doria and G. Renand collections. Private collection, Paris. Photo Hyperion.
90. SOUP. 26 by 35 cm. Private collection. Photo Druet.
SOUP. Drawing accentuated with wash, 26 by 40 cm. Musée du Louvre, Paris.
91. THE SECRET. Canvas, 26 by 35 cm. Formerly E. Blot collection. Photo Vizzavona.
HEAD OF A WOMAN. Drawing. Private collection.
92. THE BOAT-TOWER. 20 by 28 cm. Formerly Lavoignat collection. Photo Vizzavona.
THE ALARM. Quill drawing. Private collection.
93. THE BEGGARS. Canvas, 59 by 73 cm. Formerly Kapferer collection. Photo Bernheim Jeune.
THE BEGGAR-WOMAN. Drawing. Private collection.
94. THE WASHERWOMEN. Wood, 45 by 33 cm. Formerly A. Alexandre collection. Max Silberberg collection. Photo Heinrich Klette.
95. THE MARKET. Chalk drawing and water-colours, 25 by 17,5 cm. Formerly Bureau collection. Mrs. J. D. Rockefeller Junior's collection, New-York. Photo Bulloz.
96. THE BURDEN. Canvas, 117 by 95 cm. Formerly A. Alexandre and G. Petit collections. Photo Giraudon.
97. THE WASHERWOMAN. Wood, 49 by 33 cm. Formerly Bureau collection. Musée du Louvre, Paris. Photo Hyperion.
98. THE WATER-CARRIER. Canvas, 26 by 16 cm. Formerly H. Rouart collection. Barnes Foundation. Merion, Pa. Photo Druet.
99. THE HOUSE-PAINTER. Canvas, 110 by 72 cm. Formerly Hazard collection. Private collection. Photo Bulloz.
100. THE BUTCHER. Water-colour, 27 by 20 cm. Formerly Bureau collection. Fogg Art Museum, Harvard University, Cambridge, U. S. A.
101. THE PORK-BUTCHER. Water-colour, 27 by 19 cm. Gerstenberg collection. Photo Druet.
102. SAVED! Canvas, 35 by 28 cm. Formerly E. Blot collection. Photo Vizzavona.
103. BATHER. Wood, 33 by 24,5 cm. Formerly Hazard collection. Gabriel Cognac collection. Photo Gauthier.
104. CHILDREN PLAYING. Water-colour, 16 by 22 cm. Formerly Henry Lapauze collection. Mme Ch. Pomaret's collection. Photo Wildenstein.
MOTHER AND CHILD. Quill drawing accentuated with water-colours. Claude Roger-Marx collection.
105. YOUNG GIRL AND CHILD. Canvas, 65 by 55 cm. Private collection, Paris. Photo Hyperion.
106. BATHING. Wood, 24,5 by 32,5 cm. Formerly Lutz and O. Schmitz collections. Photo Druet.
STUDY OF THE NUDE. Drawing. Claude Roger-Marx collection, Paris.
107. AFTER THE BATHE. Canvas, 16,1 by 22 cm. Formerly O. Schmitz collection. Photo Wildenstein.
STUDY OF THE NUDE. Drawing. Claude Roger-Marx collection, Paris.
108. NUDE CHILDREN. 27 by 21,5 cm. Private collection. Photo Druet.
109. THE BATHERS. Canvas, 31 by 24 cm. Formerly Camontron collection. Photo Vizzavona.
110. PASSERS-BY. Canvas, 58 by 112 cm. Musée de Lyon. Photo Giraudon.

RETURNING FROM MARKET. Canvas, 37 by 29 cm. Formerly O. Schmitz collection.
111. COMPOSITION. Canvas, 22,5 by 34 cm. Private collection. Photo Bernheim Jeune.
TWO CHARACTERS. Water-colour. Claude Roger-Marx collection, Paris.
112. THE EMIGRANTS. Wood, 16 by 31 cm. W. Van Horne collection, Montreal. Photo Vizzavona.
THE EMIGRANTS. Drawing. Claude Roger-Marx collection, Paris.
113. THE EMIGRANTS. Wood, 16 by 28,5 cm. Palais des Beaux-Arts de la Ville de Paris. Photo Hyperion.
114. THE WATERING-PLACE. Wood, 44 by 55 cm. Private collection, England. Photo Gold.
CENTAUR RAVISHING A NYMPH. Drawing, 25 by 35 cm. Claude Roger-Marx collection, Paris.
115. HORSEMEN. Canvas, 60 by 85 cm. Formerly E. Blot collection. Private collection, Germany. Photo Druet.
RIDERS. Drawing. 21 by 26,5 cm. Claude Roger-Marx collection, Paris.
116. HORSEMEN IN THE FOREST. Private collection. Photo Druet.
TWO RIDERS. Drawing. Claude Roger-Marx collection, Paris.
117. SUNDAY MORNING. 18,5 by 26,5 cm. Formerly Bureau collection. David-Weill collection, Paris. Photo Gold.
LANDSCAPE. Drawing, 22 by 33 cm. Claude Roger-Marx collection, Paris.
118. THE KISS. Drawing in brown charcoal, 30 by 25 cm. Walter Gay collection, Musée du Louvre. Photo Giraudon.
119. ŒDIPUS AND THE SHEPHERD. Canvas, 65 by 50 cm. M. Silberberg collection. Photo Bulloz.
120. THE THIEVES AND THE ASS. Canvas, 59 by 56 cm. Geoffroy-Dechaume collection. Musée du Louvre. Photo Giraudon.
121. MARY MAGDALEN. Canvas, 41 by 33 cm. Formerly Cavé collection. Private collection, Paris. Photo Hyperion.
122. THE SECOND CLASS CARRIAGE. 32 by 45 cm. Formerly Forbes and Rosenberg coll. Simu Museum, Bucarest. Photo Foto-Press.
123. THE THIRD CLASS CARRIAGE. Canvas, 67 by 93 cm. Formerly A. Doria collection. Murray collection, Aberdeen. Photo Durand-Ruel.
124. THE THIRD CLASS CARRIAGE. Water-colour, 29 by 22, 5 cm. Gerstenberg collection. Photo Druet.
WAITING FOR THE TRAIN. Drawing, 22 by 16 cm. Private collection.
125. THE THIRD CLASS CARRIAGE. Wood, 25,5 by 33 cm. Private collection. Photo Bernheim Jeune.
MAN SEATED. Drawing. Claude Roger-Marx collection, Paris.
126. THE WAITING-ROOM. Painting on paper, 29 by 22,5 cm. Formerly Bureau collection. A. G. Goodyear collection, New-York. Photo Paul Rosenberg.
127. THE NIGHT-WANDERERS. Wood, 28 by 19 cm. Formerly H. Rouart collection. Photo Vizzavona.
128. ORCHESTRA STALLS. Wood, 26 by 35 cm. Chester Dale collection, New-York. Photo Vizzavona.
129. THE AUDIENCE. Water-colour, 19 by 26 cm. Formerly H. Rouart collection. Ernest Rouart collection. Photo Hyperion.
130. COMING OUT OF THE THEATRE. Canvas, 32 by 40 cm. Formerly Vollard collection. Photo Druet.
131. THE AUDIENCE. Wood, 30 by 40 cm. Formerly Tavernier collection. Photo Vizzavona.
132. THE INTERVAL. Water-colour, 27 by 35 cm. O. Reinhardt collection, Winterthür. Photo Druet.
133. AT THE THEATRE. Water-colour, 27 by 34,5 cm. Gerstenberg collection. Photo Durand-Ruel.
134. AT THE THEATRE. Wood, 21 by 27 cm. Formerly Bazard collection. Photo Vizzavona.
AT THE THEATRE. Drawing. Claude Roger-Marx collection.
135. AT THE THEATRE. 31 by 40 cm. Private collection. Photo Wildenstein.
AT THE THEATRE. Drawing, 22 by 20 cm. Private collection.
136. PIERROT PLAYING THE GUITAR. Wood, 35 by 27 cm. O. Reinhardt collection, Winterthür. Photo Gold.
137. SCENE FROM A PLAY. Wood, 31,3 by 23,2 cm. Musée du Louvre. Photo Hyperion.
138. THE DRAMA. Canvas, 97 by 89 cm. Formerly Georges Viau collection. Neue Staatsgalerie, Munich. Photo Druet.
139. A FREE SHOW. Canvas, 56 by 45 cm. Private collection. Photo Durand-Ruel.
140. THEATRE SCENE. Private collection. Photo Wildenstein.
CHARACTERS FROM MOLIÈRE. Drawing, 16 by 18 cm. Claude Roger-Marx, Paris.
141. « LE MALADE IMAGINAIRE ». Wood, 25 by 92 cm. Formerly A. Doria collection. Photo Durand-Ruel.
THE SICK MAN IN BED. Drawing, quill and wash, 12 by 22 cm. Ernest Rouart collection, Paris.

142. SCENE FROM A PLAY. Water-colour. Private collection. Photo Bernheim Jeune.
    CLOWN. Drawing. Private collection.
143. CRISPIN AND SCAPIN. Canvas, 60 by 82 cm. Formerly Daubigny and H. Rouart collections. Musée du Louvre. Photo Druet.
    CLOWN. Water-colour, 36,5 by 26 cm. Formerly Bureau collection. Metropolitan Museum, New-York.
144. HEAD OF PASQUIN. Wood, 22 by 16,5 cm. Formerly A. Doria collection. Photo Durand-Ruel.
145. CLOWN. Wood, 22 by 16 cm. Sydney W. Brown collection, Switzerland. Photo Hyperion.
146. THE MOUNTEBANKS AT REST. Canvas, 54 by 66 cm. Arthur Sachs collection, New-York. Photo Druet.
    MOUNTEBANKS. Water-colour. Claude Roger-Marx collection, Paris.
147. THE MOUNTEBANKS PARADE. 25 by 32 cm. Formerly Mme Esnault-Pelterie's collection. Photo Bulloz.
    MOUNTEBANKS. Water-colour. Claude Roger-Marx collection, Paris.
148. THE SHOW. Quill drawing on tracing paper, 38,5 by 29 cm. Private collection. Photo Durand-Ruel.
149. THE SHOW. Water-colour, 42 by 32 cm. Formerly Montrosier collection. Mme Esnault-Pelterie's collection. Photo Bulloz.
150. MOUNTEBANKS MOVING. Drawing accentuated with India-ink wash and water-colours, 38,5 by 27 cm. Hartford Museum, Connecticut, U. S. A. Photo Bulloz.
151. THE STREET-SINGERS. Water-colour, 34 by 26 cm. Formerly Jacquette collection. Palais des Beaux-Arts de la Ville de Paris. Photo Giraudon.
152. THE STRONG MAN OF THE FAIR. 25 by 35 cm. Simu Museum, Bucarest. Photo Foto-Press.
    STUDY FOR « THE MOUNTEBANKS », centre group. Photo P. Rosenberg.
153. THE SHOW. Water-colour, 26,6 by 36,7 cm. Formerly Dumas Fils and H. Rouart collections. Musée du Louvre. Photo Hyperion.
154. DON QUIXOTE. Canvas, 46 by 32 cm. Formerly Uhle collection. Neue Pinakothek, Munich. Photo Druet.
155. DON QUIXOTE AND SANCHO PANZA. Canvas, 100 by 77 cm. Formerly Vollard collection. Photo Druet.
156. DON QUIXOTE PRANCING BEFORE SANCHO PANZA. Charcoal drawing, 34 by 25 cm. Formerly Vollard collection. Photo Bulloz.
157. DON QUIXOTE IN THE MOUNTAINS. Wood, 39 by 32 cm. Robert Freat Payne collection. Photo Druet.
158. DON QUIXOTE AND SANCHO PANZA. Wood, 30 by 44 cm. O. Reinhardt collection, Winterthur. Photo Vizzavona.
    DON QUIXOTE. Drawing. Claude Roger-Marx collection, Paris.
159. DON QUIXOTE AND SANCHO PANZA. Canvas, 56 by 84 cm. Formerly Bureau collection. Mrs. C. Payson's collection, New-York.
    DON QUIXOTE AND SANCHO PANZA. Drawing. Claude Roger-Marx collection, Paris.
160. DON QUIXOTE READING. Canvas, 34 by 22,5 cm. National Gallery of Victoria, Melbourne. Photo Bernheim Jeune.

CONTENTS

Daumier as a Painter	7
Daumier the Man	11
Daumier's Achievement	20
Daumier Today	28
Bibliography	30
The Works	33
Daumier and the Critics	161
Detailed description of the plates and reproductions	166